STOKER ON STOKER

STOKER ON STOKER

Dacre Stoker

First Published in October 2019 by
Telos Publishing, 139 Whitstable Road, Canterbury, Kent
CT2 8EQ, United Kingdom

V3 April 2022

www.telos.co.uk

Telos Publishing values feedback if you have any comments about
this book please email feedback@telos.co.uk

ISBN: 978-1-84583-202-5

British Library Cataloguing in Publication Data. A catalogue record
for this book is available from the British Library.

CONTENTS

INTRODUCTION

In some ways it is a pity that Bram Stoker did not write an autobiography. If he had we would perhaps have answers to questions that scholars, biographers and fans alike have debated since *Dracula* was first published in 1897. On the other hand these unanswered questions about Bram's inspirations and hidden meanings in *Dracula* have kept the novel alive for more than a century. This is how I came to be involved in my family's legacy: I wanted to learn more about the kind of a man my great grand-uncle really was.

Harry Ludlam, a rural newspaper editor, wrote a biography of Bram Stoker in 1962, and in it he claimed that Bram was a 'most uninteresting man who wrote a most interesting story'. On the contrary, I believe that Bram was a very interesting man indeed, with a very vivid sense of imagination. He might not have been a gifted writer, but he certainly worked very hard at his writing and I believe that he loved the satisfaction of expressing himself in words, especially when I read his stories that create such a feeling of reality while delving into fantasy, supernatural and romance.

Bram was, from the available evidence, a very practical man, good with numbers and keeping everything in order, but at the same time he had a keen sense of imagination, developed through the first seven years of his life during which he was often sickly and near death. His childhood fantasies were fueled by stories rich in Irish folklore and mythology that were shared with him by both his mother and his nanny, Ellen Crone.

In this small volume I will share some of the interesting documents and ideas I have found in my own quest to understand Bram Stoker. In my own way, I play the role of a literary forensic detective: I am slowly accumulating more and more of the crucial pieces of information, which fit together like some esoteric jigsaw puzzle, to help create a clearer picture of the research that went into writing *Dracula*.

Herein you will find reproduced, the only newspaper interview I have been able to locate about Bram's writing of *Dracula*. I also include other interesting 'bits and pieces' that shed light on mysteries surrounding Bram's inspirations and his years of research for writing *Dracula*.

I hope you enjoy these notes and the factual elements I have assembled here as much as I have enjoyed searching for them in the margins of history.

Maybe the information shared here will act as springboards for other research and further information about my great grand-uncle can be revealed.

Dacre C Stoker, September 2019

BRAM STOKER, FROM MY PERSPECTIVE

'When one is conversing with him it is always intensely difficult to realise that he has been the author of that most blood curdling and thrilling of modern tales, *Dracula*.'
Antionette Sterling & Other Celebrities, MS MacKinlay 1906

Although history will always remember Bram Stoker as the author of *Dracula*, it was his *Personal Reminiscences of Henry Irving*, published in 1906 shortly after Irving's death, that won Bram acclaim during his life. Bram's employer, the most famous Shakespearean actor of his day, knighted in 1895 for services to the stage, was in modern terms, a rock star. When the two men were in public, all eyes were on the actor: Irving lived in the spotlight with Bram in the shadows. In contrast to the very private Bram, Irving's life was an open book, yet today Irving is largely unknown.

A recollection of Bram Stoker's life is not complete without considering common threads between Bram's life and *Dracula*. Reminiscent of the best Irish story telling traditions, all of Bram's fiction incorporated people and places he knew intimately, familiar stories and life situations.

In the record of his years with Irving, Bram's modest self-observations give only glimpses of himself. Fortunately, Bram recorded some aspects of his childhood as adult recollections.

But his autobiographical stories are scant, only enough to be tantalising, and obviously coloured with his great imagination. He wrote that he was a sickly child, but he made no mention of his siblings being unwell, and gave no detail of his symptoms. Considering the number of sick children in Ireland in the 1800s, Bram's infirmity may not have made a lasting impression on anyone other than himself. Significantly, his illness has never been defined, and if Bram had not made note of it, his illness may have been gone unrecorded, which would have dramatically changed modern interpretations of *Dracula*.

The possibility that Bram was bled as part of his early medical treatment is intriguing, especially as it relates to *Dracula*, but the evidence is certainly not conclusive. That sick children were subjected to, and were able to survive, the horrific processes outlined in mid-nineteenth century medical publications, may be hard for us to understand. But for some doctors, notably Abraham Stoker Sr's cousin, Dr William Stoker, bleeding was used as matter of course. Dr William Stoker died when Bram was only a year old, so any medical treatment Bram remembered, whether consciously or subconsciously would likely have been administered by William's son, Dr Edward Alexander Stoker. Purging and evacuation preceded bleeding. Maybe the children had to be sufficiently weakened before they would submit to the application of leeches, or the slice of their vein!

'Bleeding … may be practiced with safety in the youngest infant …, although they bear well one or two full bleedings, but ill endure a further repetition. We can generally however, procure as much as we require from a vein in on the dorsum of the foot, the back of the hand, or, when these fail, from the jugular vein. Leeches, can always be applied, and will take a sufficiency of blood … The quantity of blood obtained by one good leech, allowed to bleed for half an hour, may be estimated at one ounce; the gradual manner in which the blood flows, not being liable to induce sudden collapse in small children. The safest place for their application is the hand or the foot … when applied in other situations, as the chest, throat, etc leeches have led to fatal results by a continuance of hemorrhage.

'Cupping is a more definite and manageable mode of abstracting blood than leeching … The nape of the neck, or interscapular space present the best situations, being sufficiently large … and out of sight, so as to cause least alarm to the child.

'It must also not be forgotten that the ill-fed and enfeebled children of the poor will not bear bleeding to the same extent, nor require it so often as those of the more wealthy class. When a child has been blooded too largely or too frequently, an alarming state of collapse may be suddenly induced, the system not possessing in early infancy much power of rallying from depression. In this state of deficient power of reaction, the child will be observed to become extremely pale, even the colour of the iris may change, and present a paler tint; the extremities are cold, pulse feeble and frequent, breathing hurried or rattling … as a general rule, it is well to stop the flow of blood when such decided pallor takes place without waiting for actual fainting.'

> *Treatise on Fever, with observations on the practice in the fever hospital and house of recovery, in Dublin.*
> By William Stoker, MD 1815.

'When the nursery bell rang at night my mother would run to the room expecting to find me dying. All my early recollection is of being carried in people's arms and of being laid down somewhere or other on a bed or a sofa if within the house, on a rug or amid cushions on the grass if the weather was fine.'

The preceding was deleted from the original manuscript of Bram's memoir of Henry Irving. The published version follows, and in the one paragraph, Bram covers twenty years:

'I had known weakness. In my babyhood I used, I understand, to be often at the point of death. Certainly till I was about seven years old I never knew what it was to stand upright. I was naturally thoughtful and the leisure of long illness gave opportunity for many thoughts which were fruitful according to their kind in later years. This early weakness however passed away in time and I grew into a strong boy and in time enlarged to the biggest member of my family. When I was in my twentieth year I was Athletic Champion of Dublin University. When I met Irving first I was in my thirtieth year. I had been for ten years in the Civil Service and was then engaged on a dry-as-dust book on *The Duties of Clerks of Petty Sessions.* I had edited a newspaper, and had exercised my spare time in many ways. As a journalist; as a writer of short and serial stories; as a teacher. In my College days I had been Auditor of the Historical Society – a post which corresponds to the Presidency of the Union in Oxford or Cambridge – and had got medals, or certificates, for History, Composition, and Oratory. I had been President of the Philosophical Society; had got Honours in pure Mathematics. I had won numerous silver cups for races of various kinds. I had played for years in the University football team where I had received the honour of a "cap!" I was physically immensely strong. In fact, I feel justified in saying I represented in my own person something of that aim of university education *mens sana in cor pore sano.'* [A sound mind in a sound body]

Personal Reminiscences of Henry Irving (1906) Bram Stoker

Any shyness he felt as a young child was overcome during Bram's adolescence, when he found himself head and shoulders above most of the boys. He was extremely popular with students and professors, witty and charming, channelling his mother's self-assuredness.

In December 1878, Bram married the famously beautiful Florence Balcombe, in Dublin, and within a few days of their marriage, whisked her away to London, to begin his job with Irving. Oscar Wilde (with whom Florence had been romantically involved in Dublin) was also living in London, finishing up at Oxford. Oscar made the most of the drama of being jilted, too busy posturing and being clever to be truly upset by Florence's break up. There must have been no ill feelings, as the Stokers easily remained friends with Oscar, his mother 'Speranza' who was also in London, and Oscar's brother Willie, who had been Bram's friend at Trinity.

Some have described Florence as miserable in London, and jealous of Bram's life at the Lyceum, but this may not be an accurate portrayal. Although she surely regretted Bram's time being dominated by the long hours at the theatre, Florence would have known beforehand what Bram's job would require. It is widely assumed that Florence resented Irving dreadfully, and she may have. But, she was a lady and knew who 'buttered their bread', so except within the family where she felt free to vent, Florence kept her feelings about Irving to herself.

If she harboured a grudge against Henry Irving, Florence may have done so on Bram's behalf. Although he did make mistakes, Irving never made an uncalculated move, and hiring Bram was nothing short of brilliant. Bram freed Irving up to focus on what really mattered most. Irving. Bram's responsibilities at the Lyceum were expansive when the troupe was in London, and when they travelled, never-ending. Bram was in his element as the ultimate organiser, making lists, and schedules, devising ways to establish order. He attended rehearsals, and personally inspected seats, curtains, lighting, and costumes before each performance. When the doors opened, he became the charming host. He hired caterers, and rearranged tables for after-theatre parties, and greeted the guests while Irving changed from his costume. Invitations for Lyceum parties were sought after; special celebrations meant seven course meals for more than three hundred guests.

Bram wrote speeches for Irving to deliver, stood quietly while he delivered them, and joined the others in raising a glass. The morning after, Bram was the accountant, tallying the books and counting the receipts. And as Irving's secretary, he answered his mail, by his own admission up to 100 letters a day, fending requests for free tickets, interviews, parts in plays, money, photographs, and souvenirs. As it turned out, one of Bram's most important assignments was to buffer Irving from all but the chosen circle, and Irving trusted his judgment completely.

The Lyceum's leading lady, Ellen Terry would note in her memoir, 'For years he has accepted favours, obligations to, etc through Bram Stoker. Never will he acknowledge them himself, either by businesslike receipt or by any word or sign. He "lays low" like Brer Rabbit better than anyone I have ever met.' That Irving was a taker cannot be disputed. Bram was a giver, and the two were a perfect match.

The associations that the Lyceum afforded and the Stokers' circle of friends in London were exciting and glamorous, and both their social lives were active and fulfilling. Although no substitute for her husband, George Stoker or another favourite, the composer William Gilbert escorted Florence to the theatre and after-parties, and a network of Stoker and Balcombe families in London provided companionship when Bram travelled abroad. Florence certainly did not stay home and feel sorry for herself. She enjoyed acting, and took part in charity performances and as an extra if needed. She was as smart as she was lovely and easily held her own within London society circles. At home, Florence entertained in a style reminiscent of the parties Bram enjoyed in Dublin, and earned rave reviews for her teas and evening socials with impressive guest lists.

Bram was accustomed to his mother's strength and self-directing nature, so it makes sense that he appreciated Florence's poise and charming self-confidence.

A year after their marriage, Florence and Bram's son was born, christened Irving Noel Thornley Stoker, with Henry Irving chosen as a godfather. As illustrated by an entry in Bram's journal in the fall of 1880, Noel's parents were smitten:

'The baby was going into town with F— and the nurse. There was a levee on so I said to F— "You ought to take the Babe and show him to the Queen."
　'She answers, "Indeed I shall do no such thing."
　'"Why?" I asked.
　'"Because she would want to put him in her crown."
The Lost Journal of Bram Stoker © 2012

The rumour of marital discord between Bram and Florence which has been perpetuated as though it were the gospel surfaced in *The Man Who Wrote Dracula* (1975), written by Bram's (great) nephew Daniel Farson. According to Farson, his grandmother, Enid Stoker, told him Florence 'was not particularly fond' of her son, Noel. And Farson named Ann Stoker, Florence's only grandchild, as having said Florence was 'put off' by sex – which Ann denied to a subsequent biographer. With Farson as the source, allegations of Bram's possible homosexuality and/or whoremongering and Florence's frigidity are also cast in doubt.

Farson was a bitter, miserable man, having suffered many hurt feelings due to his own parents' lack of consideration, and was deeply jealous of his cousin, Noel Stoker. Sadly the rumours, half-truths, and even lies told to hurt Noel, would have brought Farson some level of satisfaction. Farson and his parents were completely dysfunctional; the title of his own autobiography, *Never a Normal Man*, summed up his life, and chronicled Farson's difficulty coming to terms with his own sexuality, alternately living asexually or as a drunk homosexual, finally dying the latter.

Noel was a quiet, shy boy, almost frail, who may have reminded Bram of his own feelings as a young child, which he recorded in his journal, several years before he and Florence married:

'I would like to steal back a moment in the twilight and whisper a prayer in some child's ear that hearing my whisper it might feel happy and no longer lonely.'

The Lost Journal of Bram Stoker © 2012

As his parents had done for their seven children, Bram provided Noel with the best education he could afford, beginning with a French governess, under whose care Noel learned to speak French before he spoke English. At eight years old, Noel went as a boarding student to Summer Fields in Oxford, a school that started boys' classical educations, and where, years later, Christopher Lee of *Dracula* movie fame, would also begin his education. After Summer Fields, Noel continued his education at prestigious Winchester College, then Oxford.

Bram included young Noel in the fun the Lyceum had to offer. The painting room at the Lyceum was the domain of Joseph Harker, (whose name was appropriated for *Dracula*) the scene painter who allowed Noel and Ellen Terry's son Gordon Craig to help him paint the Lyceum's forty-foot canvas backdrops There were other forays to the Lyceum, including this story, relayed by Bram in *Personal Reminiscences of Henry Irving*:

'When my son, who is Irving's godson, then about seven years old, came to see *Faust* I brought him round between acts to see Mephistopheles in his dressing-room. The little chap was exceedingly pretty – like a cupid – and a quaint fancy struck the actor. Telling the boy to stand still for a moment he took his dark pencil and with a few rapid touches made him up after the manner of Mephistopheles; the same high-arched eyebrows; the same sneer at the corners of the mouth; the same pointed moustache. I think it was the strangest and prettiest transformation I ever saw. And I think the child thought so too, for he was simply entranced with delight.

'Irving loved children and I think he was as enchanted over the incident as was the child himself.'

There were delightful parties for the children of the Stokers' friends, including a costume ball when Noel was ten years old, given for the daughter of the artist Mortimer Menpes, by her parents. Dancing, games and elaborate costumes on a who's who cast of London's finest miniatures. 'The youthful Noel Stoker as a "Japanese Swell", in a perfectly correct and superb costume brought from Japan, strode about with all the self-possession and staid, philosophic calm of that almond-eyed race,' reported *The Lady* on 24 January 1889.

Bram told Noel the old stories from Ireland, the fairy tales he heard as a boy from his mother and Ellen Crone. Irish fairy tales have banshees, sinking bogs, and blood sucking fairies and even if Noel did not enjoy them, Bram did. Inspired, Bram wrote *Under the Sunset*, a collection of children's stories, but the stories and the eerie illustrations may have been more appropriate for the adults who read them aloud than for the children who heard them. Reminiscent of Charlotte's stories of cholera in Sligo, in Bram's 'The Invisible Giant', an orphan girl is the heroine, and when not crying for her poor dead mother, she tries to warn her village of impending doom, the plague in the form of a cold mist, a huge shadowy form with 'grim spectral hands'. Of course the townspeople don't believe her, and she is mocked by the other children. Her goodness and innocence prevail, but not before she and her only friends, the birds and a dying old man, endure all manner of sadness and horrors.

To put his life in perspective, it helps to consider the Stoker family and Bram's Irish roots. He was only Abraham Stoker Jr – the third of Abraham and Charlotte Stoker's seven children, born on 8

First published 1881: *Under the Sunset and Other Stories*. Sampson Low, Marston, Searle and Rivington, London. Art is by W V Cockburn and accompanied a story called 'The Invisible Giant'.

November, 1847 in Clontarf during a potato famine. Ireland was not well, and neither was Bram, in fact he was not expected to live.

Living on the outskirts of Dublin provided a healthier atmosphere for the young Stoker children than the crowded city where disease was rampant. Unlike the heavy, persistent, foul odours that defined many areas of Dublin, the smell of rotting seaweed on the shore at Clontarf was dissipated by the sea breeze. The rural feel of suburban Killester and Artane, where the Stokers would move before Bram was two years old was absolute heaven in contrast to the scene in Dublin; poor people, living hand to mouth in unsanitary conditions; beggars with their clothes rotting off their rotting bodies. Abraham and Charlotte felt compassion for the Irish peasants, stuck as they were in a hopeless cycle of famine, starvation and disease, but their compassion would not have quelled the very real fear that disease would strike within their own family.

Ireland's population was in decline due to disease, starvation, and mass emigration. But, as the country shrank, Dublin grew, and boatloads of emigrants telling stories of the horrors they left behind, helped establish Dublin's reputation for having some of the worst living conditions in all of Europe.

The rural peasants who did not flee Ireland, flooded into Dublin. They dragged themselves away from the ravaged countryside, where every stick and straw had been stripped to build fires for warmth and to boil the kettles. When lucky, their kettle included a few oats to make thin skilly, if not, the fare was simply blades of grass boiled in water. So, like children looking to parents for assistance, Ireland's poor came seeking work and refuge in Dublin. But, in contrast to the prosperous city of Belfast, with its shipbuilding and linen industries, Dublin had no great source of employment.

My great-great grandfather (Bram's father) Abraham Sr was fortunate. He was sixteen in 1815 when he began work as a clerk in the Chief Secretary's Office at Dublin Castle, before the really hard times hit Ireland. Until Irish Independence in 1922, the Castle was the residence of the Lord Lieutenant of Ireland, the English Monarch's representative. The Chief Secretary was second in command to the Lord Lieutenant, and his office handled all communication and correspondence between English governmental agencies and their Irish counterparts. As a clerk, Abraham's work was endless, rooms full of papers to catalogue according to a complex filing system;

documents ranging from the mundane day-to-day business of the country to official responses to famine, poverty, disease epidemics, prisons, hospitals, rebellion, and political unrest. If Abraham wanted to ignore the horrors facing Ireland, he could not have. Perhaps as a thoughtful and calculated consequence, Abraham did not marry until he was forty-four years old, after twenty-eight years of work and a certain feeling of job security. He retired after fifty years (in 1865) with a pension equal to his annual salary.

My great-great grandmother (Bram's mother) Charlotte Matilda Thornley was nineteen years younger than her husband, Abraham, a divide comparable to her own parents' age difference. Although Charlotte's family was not wealthy by any means, her mother's family, the Blakes of Garracloon were part of an expansive Blake family tree, branches of which still owned thousands of acres from an original grant. Charlotte came to her marriage in 1844 bringing furniture for the house in Clontarf, and incredible self-assurance, both which her descendants still possess.

Charlotte grew up in Sligo in the northwest of Ireland, her childhood defined by horrors of the Cholera epidemic. If she had not written the stories down so vividly, one might wonder if Bram made them up. People were buried before they were dead; crawling from their graves. If a patient was in an opium stupor, he might be taken as dead – and taken away to clear space for the next patient; one man was awakened from a blow meant to break his legs to him fit into a small coffin. Charlotte's true stories were more horrible than Bram's fiction, and the similarities are undeniable.

Charlotte was a storyteller who knew how to keep a bed-ridden young boy entertained. But, in the bigger picture, she was an intelligent and strong-willed woman from a religious family. As a married woman she had virtually no rights; Charlotte, her property and her children legally belonged to Abraham, but her voice was her own. Although he was old enough to be her father, Abraham must have had enormous respect for Charlotte. Charlotte advocated for women's rights, she was passionate and outspoken on issues such as fair labour laws, working conditions in poor houses, and the need to educate the deaf and dumb. The Stoker family motto, 'whatever is right and honorable', defined Abraham and Charlotte's own ideals and the path they set forth for their seven children.

At the time, families who could afford it, employed nurses as primary caregivers for infants, thus mothers could resist becoming too attached in case the babies fell ill and died. But, unless a mother was physically unable to nurse her infant, employing a wet nurse was an upper class vanity. There is nothing to suggest that anyone other than Charlotte nursed the Stoker children, and Ellen Crone, the nurse who lived with and cared for all seven of the Stoker children, was closer in age to Abraham Sr than to Charlotte. Although in fairy tales a 'crone' is an evil old woman with supernatural powers, Ellen used whatever powers she had to the benefit of her charges and all seven children survived. Ellen remained close to the family members in Dublin until her death in 1869 at sixty eight years old, and was memorialised by Bram's eldest brother, Thornley, with a plaque in the graveyard at Rathmines, 'for many years the devoted nurse and friend in the family of Abraham and Charlotte Stoker, and in whose services she died.' A lock of Ellen's hair kept as a treasure by Thornley Stoker and deposited after his death in a Dublin collection, survives today.

Though Abraham and Charlotte surely struggled to afford their children's educational expenses, their efforts paid off. Considering their parents' humble beginnings, the level of success the seven children attained cannot be overstated. The two Stoker daughters were young ladies, well-read, well-travelled, and properly schooled in the fine arts. And, with successful civil service, military, and medical careers, each of the five Stoker boys established themselves professionally, and socially.

The eldest Stoker sibling, William Thornley, was born in Clontarf in 1845, the year after his parents' marriage. Thornley was educated at the Grammar School, a day and boarding school at Wymondham, Norfolk, England; Dublin's Royal College of Surgeons; and the Queen's College, Galway, Ireland. Thornley was a philanthropist, and took up his mother's cause against the evils of the workhouse system, the grievances of doctors who ministered to the poor, and the prevention of cruelty to animals.

Thornley's professional resume was both lengthy and impressive, the details of which space does not allow. He was a professor of anatomy, and served as a surgeon and on the board of a number of Dublin Hospitals, and as president of the Royal College of Surgeons of Ireland in 1894 and 1895, and from 1903 to 1906, President of the Royal Academy of Surgeons. Thornley and his wife, Emily married in

1875, when he was thirty, and she two years younger. They had no children, but opened their home to nieces and nephews. As Thornley's star rose, both professionally and socially, they moved from Dublin's Harcourt Street, to Ely House, a handsome, antique-filled Georgian House. Lady Emily's physical and mental health was in serious decline after 1906. She was cared for at home for a few years, but was institutionalised in 1910, and passed away in November of that year.

Thornley served as surgeon to Swift's Hospital for Lunatics, and herein lies his connection to *Dracula*, and the likelihood that the Bram based the character of Dr Abraham Van Helsing on his eldest brother. Thornley sketched and outlined notes in some detail for Bram, detailing a brain injury such as Renfield's. The notes, which are in the collection at the Rosenbach Museum are similar to medical papers Thornley presented as early as the 1870's, describing brain injuries, surgical techniques, treatment and recovery. Amongst his many accolades, Thornley was remembered for being a pioneer, performing certain surgeries before there were even names for what he was doing. In recognition of his years of service, he was knighted in 1895 and further honored with a Baronetcy the year before his death.

The obituary in the British Medical Journal, 15 June, 1912 summarises the significance of this very special man. 'He was an earnest student of literature and a keen critic of style. His professional writings were forceful and terse, while his private letters show a mastery of elegant English. He was an acknowledged authority on questions of art, and had an unerring judgment of the artistic values of form, colour, and material. But however one may speak of his professional eminence, his literary, artistic, and social proclivities, yet, when all is said, one has scarcely touched the man himself-intensely human, entirely lovable, genial, sympathetic, and great hearted.'

Bram was very close to his sister Matilda, who was just one year older than he. She was educated at the Dublin Art School, and was a member of the Royal Hibernian Academy, studying painting and ceramics. She and her younger sister, Margaret, went abroad with their parents when Abraham Sr retired, first to France, then Switzerland, and Italy, where Matilda continued to study art. Matilda moved to London soon after her father died, and lived first with Bram and Florence, then with youngest Stoker brother, George and his wife Agnes. In 1889, at the age of 43 she married Charles Auguste Petitjean, eleven years her junior. He shared Matilda's appreciation of art, co-authoring *Catalogue of the Engraved Portraits by Jean Morin* (c.1590 – 1650) with Murray Hornibrook, the husband of her sister Margaret's daughter, Gladys.

Thomas, born in 1849 was the first of the three youngest Stoker boys to attend Dr Benson's Rathmines School. An educational journal described Rathmines School: 'Boys are prepared for the diversities, the Royal College of Surgeons, the Examination for Solicitors' Apprentices, the Banks, or for Commercial life. There are also classes for the Examinations held under the Intermediate Education Act.'

Charles Benson, the school's founder and headmaster was an Anglican priest, who inspired many of his students to the priesthood and as missionaries. A keen naturalist, and an Honorary Member of the Royal Zoological Society Ireland, he instilled of a life-long love of God's handiwork, nature and the outdoors in his students, including the Stoker boys. After Rathmines School, Tom excelled at Trinity College, after which he was appointed to the Bengal civil service and over the years served as Deputy Superintendent of family domains of Maharaja of Benares, District and Settlement Officer, and Chief Secretary of Government, North West Provinces and Oudh.

In 1891, Tom returned to Dublin to marry Enid Bruce, twenty-five years his junior, whose father, William R Bruce, KC [King's Counsel] was Master of the King's Bench. Eight years later, Tom retired to London with Enid and their daughter, Eve, born in 1893 in West Bengal. Shortly after his retirement, Tom published a collection of short stories, with his life in India as a backdrop. His references to 'field sports and manly exercises', pig-hunting on horseback, bird shooting, polo, and the Turf Club provide a picture of him and his life in India that otherwise could not have been imagined. His story, 'The Justice of the Raj' features a kindly English inspector, a sportsman with a wife and six-year-old daughter, Evie, who bear a strong resemblance to Tom's own wife and daughter Eve. Long suffering from asthma, Tom's health deteriorated after his retirement in 1899. Blind for the last nine years of his life, he died in 1925, two months before his seventy sixth birthday.

The fifth Stoker child, Richard Nugent, born in 1851, was named in honour of Edmund Nugent, the Anglican priest who baptised each of the Stoker children. Richard, or 'Dick', attended Rathmines School and like Thornley studied at the Royal College of Surgeons. He was licensed by King's and Queen's College of Physicians in 1874, and joined the India Medical Services. In 1875, Dick married Susan Harden, the beautiful, blue-eyed niece of Dr Benson, the Rathmines' headmaster. Susan had studied china painting and watercolours at the Dublin School of Art, and was herself a naturalist. She went with Dick to live in the mountains of North West India for twenty years. Their one child did not survive, he or she was either stillborn, or died as an infant in India. Keen botanists and fascinated by what they found in India, Dick and Susan both collected seeds and plant specimens and sketched and painted the natural world around them. Susan's watercolours of butterflies and moths show detailed colour, executed with the eye of an entomologist and simply signed with 'SS'. Dick's sketches and paintings were rendered with an artist's hand and an Irish sense of humour. He did not seem to take his task as seriously as his wife, labeling his work casually: 'A grass cricket half painted, for he would not stay quiet', 'Cockroaches, they are very common in the houses', 'Lots of these beetles on the roads', 'Flying bug of some sort'.

Dick preferred the more secluded outposts, where he was free to hunt and fish, and had time to record the specimens he took. Some of which he contributed to *Stray Feathers: Journal of Ornithology for India and its Dependencies*, Vol 10, 1887, edited by Allan Hume, ornithological expert and founding father of the Indian National Congress.

Dick was made Surgeon Lieutenant Colonel in 1894, six years before his retirement. Dick and Susan planned to relocate to Tasmania when he retired, but while travelling, they fell in love with the wilderness of British Columbia, Canada and bought acreage. They returned to Canada in 1900 and spent their summers in a log cabin on Lake Cowichan where Dick continued to hunt and fish and the couple established a vast, naturally landscaped rhododendron garden which still exists. Until his death in 1931, and hers in 1936 the long Canadian winters were spent in a comfortable, two-storey, white clapboard house they built in the nearby town of Maple Bay,

Margaret Dalrymple Stoker, born in 1853, was just twelve when her father retired, and fifteen when Bram began work at Dublin Castle. She and Matilda went abroad to live with their parents in 1872, where they could all live more cheaply on Abraham's retirement fund. The family originally planned to travel to France and Switzerland, but would add Italy to the agenda as well, to round out the girls' education. After Abraham Sr's death in Naples in 1876, both daughters remained with Charlotte in Italy for a time. Margaret returned to Dublin to live with Thornley and Emily, before marrying William Thomson, a physician, surgeon, associate and neighbour on Harcourt Street. Thomson's medical career was impressive, his obituary would list accomplishments and recognitions to rival Thornley's, including being knighted in 1897, and awarded a Baronetcy in 1900.

During the Boer War, Margaret (by then, Lady Thomson) coordinated charity drives in Dublin to gather gifts and supplies to send to South Africa, while her husband served as Chief Surgeon to the Irish Hospital in South Africa, and son, Douglas, served as a dresser, or junior medical staff.

Like his brothers Richard and Tom, the youngest Stoker, my great grandfather, George, attended Dr Benson's Rathmines School, before he followed Thornley and Richard to the Royal College of Physicians and then joined the Irish Medical Corps. As one of many of the good Samaritans who stepped in to help during the Russo-Turkish war from 1876 to 78, George joined the medical department of the Turkish Army, when the National Aid Society (later the Red Cross) determined to send impartial medical aid to both sides.

George's own book *With 'the Unspeakables'; or Two Years Campaigning in European and Asiatic Turkey* (Chapman & Hall, 1878), as well as first-hand accounts by others, describe in detail the Balkan Mountains near the Shipka Pass, where he arranged transportation for the wounded from the battlefields by mule drawn ambulances, down to hospitals at Adrianople and Phillippolos.

This Balkan region was unknown to Bram in all his travels, yet the realism in Jonathan Harker's travelogue through Romania and the Carpathian Mountains cannot be denied. George's written descriptions of the mountains and the people are vivid, and with George and Bram both living in London during the seven years Bram researched and wrote *Dracula*, it is easy to imagine the conversations between the brothers and the extent to which George's experiences in the Balkans influenced Bram's descriptions of the scenery and the gypsies in Transylvania.

In his book George reflected on his two years in Turkey: 'the never-ending slavery, the hard, ceaseless grinding drudgery which had to be endured by surgeons in the late war. With imperfect arrangements, imperfect appliances, deficient food and manual help, and with the heart-sickening feeling that all was in a state of confusion which might at any moment tend to hopeless disaster, our days and nights wore on.'

In addition to ambulance operations, George was in charge of setting up one of four relief hospitals, which was met by Turkish skepticism, as villagers were convinced the large house was being converted to either a brothel or a madhouse. On one occasion he went to Phillippolos, and the events were described by Dorothy Anderson in *The Balkan Volunteers* (1968): 'to escort English nurses to their posts. Two were to go to the hospital at Batak, and the journey there proved a hazardous expedition. One of the nurses weighed sixteen stone, and there was first the problem of finding a horse robust enough to carry her, and then the difficulty of keeping her on it over the icy and precipitous paths. One *zaptieh* led the horse, two more, one on each side, kept the nurse upright, and Stoker in the rear, cheerful and encouraging as always, pushed. There was no need of that encouragement with the cold and the snow and the wolfpacks.'

George continued to serve with The Stafford House Surgeons during the Zulu Wars in South Africa, becoming in 1879, the Commissioner of the South African aid committee.

He also served in the Boer War, as second-in-command to his brother-in-law, Sir William Thomson, Chief Surgeon of the Irish Hospital, South African Field Force.

Upon returning to London, George became a distinguished Otologist at the London Throat Hospital, before starting the London Ozone Hospital, under the patronage of Princess Louise. His papers on the Surgical Uses and the Healing Properties of Ozone, are still referenced today.

In 1884, George married Agnes McGillycuddy, one of seventeen children of Richard, the McGillycuddy of the Reeks in County Kerry. Their two children were born in London, but for a number of years, George and Agnes divided their time between England and in County Kerry, Ireland, where they leased Dunloe Castle.

Minna, the governess who lived with my great grandparents, Agnes and George Stoker, and my grandfather, Tom and his sister had her name appropriated by Bram for his character, Mina Murray, a school mistress – one of the many overlaps between Bram Stoker's own life, and his fiction.

In all his fiction, Bram wrote what he felt and about the people he knew; and was adept at weaving his imagination with past, present, and future realities, leaving the reader unsure how to distinguish between reality and Bram's fabrications.

The reality is that 125 years after the publication of *Dracula*, interest in Bram's inspirations for writing his classic novel is at an all-time high. The unknown or undefined aspects of *Dracula* leave the book and Bram's intent open to speculation. Consequently, many careers have been built on clever re-imaginings of his vampire in fiction and commerce.

As a shape-shifter extraordinaire, the character of Count Dracula invites constant reinterpretation and reinvention. The evolution of Dracula keeps him alive.

IRVING NOEL THORNLEY STOKER

Richard Noel Dobbs

My grandparents Noel (full name Irving Noel Thornley Stoker, son of Bram Stoker) and Neelie were married in 1910 and remained happily married for 50 years: they had an only child, Ann – my mother, born in 1916. She married my father (a Royal Navy pilot) in 1936. I was born in 1937 followed a year later by my brother Jamie. Our father was killed in 1939 in a flying accident – practising torpedo runs at night off an aircraft carrier in the Mediterranean. Our mother became a widow at the age of twenty two with two young children. I do not know the details, but from then on effectively our grandparents took over responsibility for Jamie and my upbringing and education, with enormous generosity and affection. Our mother remarried and they had one son, Robin MacCaw, my half-brother: this marriage did not last.

When Bram arrived in London from Dublin to work for Henry Irving in 1878, having recently married Florence, he was new to London and English 'society': however his contacts through the theatre enabled him to send his son Noel to the 'right' schools, Summer Fields Preparatory and Winchester College (founded in 1381). Noel then went to New College, the Oxford college founded by William of Wykeham. Noel paid for all of Jamie and my private education including Winchester in his old House, which I think gave him a lot of pleasure, particularly as we both played Winchester College football, as he had nearly 60 years previously. I always said I was educated thanks to *Dracula*. Bram's contacts also enabled him to arrange for Noel to become an apprentice to the Skinners Company, where he enjoyed dining for 50 years.

The Skinners were originally the furriers and were founded in 1327 and are one of the 'Great Twelve Livery Companies' of the City of London. Both Jamie and I became Skinners and I was Master in 1989-90. I think Bram was aware that he was neglecting his son for the sake of his position with Irving so was trying to compensate by arranging first class education and membership of the Skinners Company.

Following the Lyceum's financial difficulties Bram's income dropped, and Noel did not want to be a financial burden, so left Oxford and became Articled to a firm of Chartered Accountants. After qualification he became a partner in Williams Stoker & Co, whose office was at 9 Bedford Row in Holborn. The firm flourished under Noel, acquiring such clients as Hoovers, the descendants of Isaac Singer's investment companies and Royce, one half of Rolls Royce. He very much had his own style and set Article Clerks an 'exam' based on questions from *The Wrong Box* by Robert Louis Stevenson.

During the 1939-45 War, Jamie and I were cared for by our grandmother Neelie, with the help of a local sixteen year-old girl who was awaiting training to be a nurse, in Seaview, Isle of Wight (where my wife Susan and I now live). We slept in a Morrison shelter, the indoor air raid shelter and were untroubled by the German bombers flying over, bound for Portsmouth, Southampton and other targets. We were almost oblivious of the war which had necessitated Noel moving his office out of London to Haslemere, in easy reach of the Isle of Wight, where he came at weekends. Jamie and I had a blissful War protected by our grandparents and playing on the beach, often picking up anti-aircraft gun shrapnel, apparently ignorant of any danger.

After the War we returned to our grandparents' house in South Kensington, London, where we spent quite a short time before commencing ten years of boarding education with holidays in Seaview. Noel spent his month-long summer holiday there also, but I am hazy if he came down at weekends. He continued to go to the office where he had a number of favourite clients he looked after: this continued until he was nearly 80, by which time Jamie and I had commenced Articles: in my case after two years military service, whilst Jamie was 'deferred' so was never called up. Noel was a dog lover and had a series of ill-trained Pekingese. I remember his walks round Seaview planned to avoid meeting certain people.

Noel had experienced poor health for a number of years: I remember being summoned back from Germany, where I was doing my military service, in 1956 as he was not expected to live: but he survived until 1961. He was philosophical and continued his life calmly and without complaint.

Although he was often away, I believe that Bram had considerable influence on his son, an only child of busy parents: Bram worked incredibly hard for a difficult and demanding man, Henry Irving. He organised eight tours of the Lyceum Company to the United States with costumes and sets, including the Atlantic crossings, hotels and trains, by his own estimate, writing by hand up to one hundred letters a day to make the arrangements. Each tour lasted up to six months and these were largely taking place during his son's teenage years, which added to the time Noel was away at boarding school must have made Bram a remote figure. Florence did not join Bram on his tours, but had a social busy life in London: perhaps her relationship with her son was exemplified by the *Punch* cartoon, where a small boy answers his mother's 'little boys should be seen and not heard' with 'but Mama you don't look at me'. As a child Noel had a French Governess and as a result spoke and read French fluently, enjoying French novels all his life. He seems to have been fond of her. I believe Florence and Noel resented Irving because of his demands on their husband/father, with the result that Noel dropped 'Irving' as his first Christian name.

Probably because of his parents' busy lives, Noel became happy and content in his own company with his books and hobbies: the hobby I best remember is his collecting of used railway tickets, which at that time were printed on small cards: return journeys were on the same card and the outward journey would be torn off to leave just the return half. He repaired the half he had collected with a blank, using a predecessor of Sellotape. The repaired tickets were then stored in custom-made cabinets. He acquired these used tickets and ticket stubs by befriending the actual ticket collectors: I never heard his 'chat up' lines but I imagine that they were taken by his old world charm and his behaviour as a perfect Edwardian gentleman. He was interested in railways and timetables for planning journeys.

Another solitary hobby, which I think took place between the Wars, was the research at the Records Office into naval history through researching ships logs: I do not know anything more than he typed up the results and these notes were then filed in loose-leaf files.

He loved reading and collecting books: I have a number of these, some perhaps inherited from his parents, in sets of Bronte, Kipling and Stevenson: also, some fine leather bound novels by Walter Scott, which he used to read to me when I was about nine. I remember how he took me for a week's holiday to Crianlarich, a village in Scotland on the edge of Loch Lomond, at about that time, when we sat up in the overnight train. I think he gave me Bram's cloak to keep me covered during the journey. Prodigious reading was not confined to English literature, but included detective stories by Ngaio Marsh and Margery Allingham, both of which had a 'gentleman' detective like Dorothy Sayers' Lord Peter Wimsey.

Noel was a gentle, kind and generous man, who was clearly very fond of Jamie and me and our father – who was an 'action man' and good athlete like Bram.

'Our grandfather' was a tall slender man with hair tinged in red, like his father. Because of his love of France and all things French he used a cummerbund to support his trousers and espadrilles as slippers. He always wore a hat and smoked a pipe and French cigarettes. He read the *Daily Telegraph* and did the crossword: boycotting *The Times* because that paper had published a poor review of *Dracula*. He talked seldom about his father or *Dracula*, although at that time there was not the same interest as today. He never drove a car or watched TV. I do not remember him listening to the 'wireless', although he may have during the war.

He and Neelie undertook caring for two small boys when they were about 60 and 54 years old respectively – probably today equivalent to 75 and 70, with selfless generosity. With the benefit of hindsight, he was the perfect gentleman as in the Winchester College motto 'Manners makyth man': he would never keep his hat on indoors and ladies would always have doors opened for them.

BRAM STOKER AND CRUDEN BAY

Mike Shepherd

Bram Stoker saw Cruden Bay for the first time in the summer of 1892 while on a walking tour of the Aberdeenshire coast in north east Scotland. 'When first I saw the place I fell in love with it,' he wrote. 'The next year I came again, and the next, and the next.' It was as if he personally injected himself into his novel *The Mystery of the Sea* which he set in the area.

Cruden Bay was at that time called Port Erroll in honour of the local aristocrat, the Earl of Erroll, who was the resident of nearby Slains Castle. Bram is known to have visited the area at least thirteen times between 1892 and 1910. A part-time author for most of his life, his holidays to Cruden Bay gave him a month-long summer break from his job as the business manager of the Lyceum Theatre in London. Bram now had the time to do exactly what he wanted, to write his books in a place of peace and quiet. He was 45 years old on his first visit, and thereafter the books came tumbling out of him.

He told a local resident that he got all the ideas for his stories while walking the coastline around Cruden Bay. And in 1895, according to his biographer Harry Ludlam, he started writing *Dracula* here. The Cruden Bay area also provided the setting for two of his novels, *The Watter's Mou'* and *The Mystery of the Sea*.

In the 1890s Port Erroll (Cruden Bay) was a small fishing village with a population of 487. It might seem astonishing that Bram Stoker would pick a tiny village on the Aberdeenshire coast for his annual summer holiday. Over 500 miles from London, it took a fourteen hour journey to get there. Not only that, Bram Stoker mixed with the elite of London society in his job at the Lyceum Theatre, and would be expected to take the waters in a fashionable European spa resort rather than spend his one holiday of the year in a remote Aberdeenshire fishing village.

A hint of an explanation comes from the words of the main character Esse in his novel *The Shoulder of Shasta*, published after his second visit north. Esse is not 'in any way addicted to society life,' instead she longed 'for the wilderness'. Bram revelled in the natural scenery of Cruden Bay. His writings suggest that he connected to nature here.

The beauty of the area is in its coastal scenery with spectacular cliffs and deserted beaches. Inland the vista is mostly mile after mile of farmer's fields. It's the walk along the coast that brings you close to nature much as Bram Stoker found it. You find yourself alone with the birds and seals, whether walking along the dune-fringed Cruden Bay beach or the rugged cliff tops beyond.

IN THE FOOTSTEPS OF BRAM STOKER: WALKS AROUND CRUDEN BAY

Walk One: Hilton Cottage to Port Erroll Harbour (walking distance: one mile)

Hilton Cottage. The starting point for this walk is Hilton Cottage, located on the left-hand side at the top of Bridge Street, 200 metres from the Kilmarnock Arms Hotel. Bram used Hilton Cottage as his main residence in Cruden Bay, probably from 1896 onwards. Hilton Cottage is a private residence – please respect the owner's privacy and do not enter the property.

The cottage was built in 1895 by James Cruickshank, owner of the Kilmarnock Arms Hotel. It's a two-story villa constructed out of red Peterhead granite. Located at the top of a broad ridge, a panoramic view is seen from here over the village of Cruden Bay and the sea beyond. The left-hand side of the villa was used as a staff residence for the hotel under the name Lilybank Cottage. Hilton Cottage comprised the right-hand-side of the villa and was used as an annexe for hotel guests. It was occupied by the Cruickshank family off-season. Today, the two halves have been merged into one residence, which retains the name Hilton Cottage.

Bram Stoker was often spotted by the villagers writing on fine summer days at a round table in the garden at Hilton Cottage. The prospect from Hilton Cottage provided Bram with what Dacre Stoker calls his visual palette. From the garden he could see Slains Castle, Port Erroll harbour, the sand dunes, the Kilmarnock Arms Hotel, and on the far horizon, the village of Whinnyfold. It's possible that he worked on the last chapters of *Dracula* here in 1896, and then on the paperback version in 1900.

Bram Stoker kept a bicycle at Hilton Cottage which was the marvel of the villagers who saw it as he cycled along the roads and across the beach. According to local resident Sandy Cruickshank it had 'stays all over the place and an upright saddle shaped like a hammock'. The journalist and cycling enthusiast Gordon Casely, who interviewed Sandy in 1966, recognised the make as a Dursley Pedersen with its distinctive cantilever frame and hammock-style saddle. The design made it easier to ride over the bumpy roads of the time.

At the start of his summer visit to Port Erroll in 1903, Bram arrived in the village with a dog. Who owned the dog is not known. He was then told that the Kilmarnock Arms Hotel enforced a strict no-pets policy in its rooms, and this included the Hilton Cottage annexe. He was obliged to ask around the village to see if anyone would look after the dog for a month.

He knocked on the door of Clifton Cottage, just along from Hilton Cottage. The servants of the house were more than happy to look after the dog. I was told by their daughter, Marna Cruickshank, that Bram Stoker was very grateful and sent her parents a big box of chocolates when he returned to London. 'I remember the chocolate box well,' Marna told me. 'It had beautiful silk violets on the front of it'.

Roselea Cottage: Further down Bridge Street you will pass Roselea Cottage on the right-hand side. Bram Stoker is known to have stayed here when everywhere else in the village was full. This was probably in the early 1900s when Cruden Bay underwent a short-lived tourist boom.

Kilmarnock Arms Hotel: Bram Stoker is known to have stayed here three times; the first visit in 1892. He signed the hotel guestbook at the start of his visits in 1894 and 1895. The 1894 entry reads: 'Second visit to Port Erroll. Delighted with everything & everybody & hope to come again to the Kilmarnock Arms'. The hotel is the only location where Bram is known for sure to have written *Dracula*.

The Kilmarnock Arms Hotel was built in 1877 and was named in honour of the Earl of Erroll's father who sat in the British House of Lords as Baron Kilmarnock. The Kilmarnock name stems from the father of the 15th Earl of Erroll, who was the fourth and last Earl of Kilmarnock. He was beheaded in 1746 on Tower Hill, London, following his capture at the Battle of Culloden where he had fought on the Jacobite side. His son, with a choice of titles to choose from, became the Earl of Erroll probably because it also made him the High Constable of Scotland.

The hotel is a two-storey building built out of red granite on an L-shaped plan. The shorter arm faces onto Bridge Street with three bay windows; the longer side with five bay windows looks over the front lawn and the Water of Cruden. An attractive motif separates the windows between the ground and upper floor, a horizontal strip made up of black and white diamonds. The crest of the Earl of Kilmarnock is displayed in white and green on the side facing Bridge Street.

An 1896 advertisement gives an idea of what the hotel was like in Bram Stoker's day:

> THIS HOTEL contains 12 Bedrooms, 2 Bathrooms (hot and cold water), Sitting Rooms, Dining Hall, etc; and is admirably adapted for small parties or families. Excellent Bathing Beach within seven minutes' walk; Bathing Houses for use of Visitors. All Visitors may have Trout Fishing in Cruden Water free of charge. There is good sea Fishing, and boats may be had for hire, also a good Golf Course. The proprietor is Lessee of over 6000 acres of Shooting (well stocked with low ground Game, which includes a small Grouse shooting). Gentlemen residing at the Hotel may have Shooting by previous arrangement, with use of dogs, etc, on reasonable terms. Horses and Machines kept for hire. Postal and Telegraph Office in the Hotel.

The location of the post office in the hotel was convenient for Bram Stoker (today it's the public bar). The post arrived daily by the horse-drawn mail gig from the nearby town of Ellon at 11am. The gig passed back through the village again at 3pm and collected outgoing mail on the return journey. The postmistress, Mrs Cruickshank, later recalled, 'Bram himself had a fine sense of humour, always joking about something. I met him quite a lot as he was always getting telegrams and letters from the Lyceum Theatre.' The door of the post office was left open during the summer and Mrs Cruickshank would shout a greeting to Bram and Florence if she saw them passing by.

Have a look inside the hotel. The reception area gives you the typical ambience of a Scottish hotel with its stag's head staring at you as you enter and a roaring log fire along one side. On the wall is a photo of the former owner James Cruickshank and a close friend of Bram Stoker. The dining room on the left-hand side is much as Bram Stoker knew it.

Bram described the breakfast fare there back in the day – a smoked haddock on his plate, and one that would have been caught and smoked by the local fisherfolk. In 1906 he opened a flower show in the nearby town of Peterhead. At the start of the speech the author professed his great love for this part of Scotland, 'which he had visited for many years. He hoped to come there as long as he lived', he said, mentioning to laughter and applause his intention 'to live on herrings all the time'.

The bridge next to the hotel is where the dramatic opening scene of *The Mystery of the Sea* is set. The hero of the novel, Archibald Hunter, is sitting here when he notices a funeral procession passing down the road in front of him. Across the road stands the mystic old woman Gormala who stares intently at him. What Archibald Hunter is about to find out is that he has the second sight, and that he has foreseen the funeral procession which will take place later that day.

Main Street: Cross the road and walk down Main Street on the way to the harbour. Formerly known as The Terrace, this was where the tradesmen of the village lived. They kept themselves separate from the fishing community who lived in the Harbour

Street area further along. Up a side street is the Port Erroll Village Hall which was opened in 1896. Here, in 1900, Bram Stoker gave a recital at a concert given by visitors to the village.

On the right-hand side is a single-story building currently in use as a newsagent and general store. Built in 1897, the year *Dracula* was published, it housed three shops including a boot maker shop run by Jimmy Beagrie. Jimmy as well as running his shop was also Bram's chauffeur when he arrived at the railway station, and would bring Bram, Florence, and their luggage to wherever he was staying.

Harbour Street and the fishing village: A bit further on is Harbour Street, which together with four side roads, makes up the former fishing village. This is how Bram described it:

'The village, squatted beside the emboucher of the Water of Cruden at the northern side of the bay is simple enough, a few rows of fishermen's cottages, two or three great red-tiled drying sheds nestled in the sand-heap behind the fishers' houses.'

The houses are of two types, the larger two-story cottages with dormer windows and the single storey 'but and bens'. The latter comprised two rooms, essentially a kitchen and a bedroom. The floors were uncarpeted, and sand was used for the covering. The fisherwoman's job every morning was to brush up the sand and replace it with a new supply from the beach. Two but and bens survive close to their original form in Green Street with their red pantile roofs topped by Victorian chimney pots.

The fishing village was overcrowded and a population of 300 persons lived here. Some of the houses held as many as twelve occupants. The two rooms of the single storey house at 5 Harbour Street held eleven members of the Summers family according to the 1891 census. It was said that in the smaller houses the occupants scarcely had enough space to breathe.

Bram was friendly with the fisherman and quickly picked up their distinctive Doric dialect. His 1895 novel *The Watter's Mou'* gives a sympathetic account of the lives of the fisherfolk. It was a hard life for the men and women. The men risked their lives every time they went out to sea. The women, apart from their domestic duties, spent hours baiting the fishing lines for the next day's catch. Bram would often see them in front of their cottages, chatting to their neighbours while working or singing songs to while away the time.

The fisherfolk were very superstitious and many of their traditions were pre-Christian in origin (pagan). Although they were deeply religious, once out at sea they would revert to the pagan attitudes of old. It was taboo to mention anything to do with the Christian religion such as a minister or a church while out in a boat. Bram Stoker took the old pagan beliefs seriously. He wrote in one of his non-fiction books that 'in times when primitivity holds sway, we are most in touch with the loftiest things we are capable of understanding …' And in *Dracula*, Van Helsing asks, 'Is there fate amongst us still, sent down from the pagan world of old …?'

The view opens up at the far end of Harbour Street with Cruden Bay beach now to be seen on the right-hand side. Behind the sandy strand are the dunes and their lime-green coat of marram grass. Here too is the estuary of the Water of Cruden, 'it runs to the sea over a stony bottom,' wrote Bram Stoker. 'The estuary has in its wash some dangerous outcropping granite rocks, nearly covered at high tide, and the mouth opens between the most northerly end of the sandhills and the village street …'

The road bends in response to a short dogleg in the ancient cliff line that lies behind the houses. Here the slope is gentle enough to carry a rough track up to a grassy area known as Ward Hill. A small house once overlooked the cliff here, and a bit further on is where the tiny coastguard lookout station was located. It can be found at the far south-eastern corner where a few granite blocks mark the outline of the hut's foundations. Bram Stoker spent many hours chatting to the coastguards on look-out duty at the hut, hearing all the gossip about the village in turn. The coastguard's names are recorded in the 1891 census; Frederick Dyson from Leeds and Walter Heron who is listed as having been born in England. The opening scene of *The Watter's Mou* is set in the coastguard hut.

Port Erroll Harbour: Round the far side of the bend in the road are a small cluster of buildings: the Salmon Bothy on the right-hand side and the single-story building of the Rocket House on the left-hand side (mentioned in *The Watter's Mou'*). The Board of

Trade life-saving apparatus was stored in the Rocket House; hefty rockets which could be fired towards any ship stranded on the rocks around Cruden Bay; a rope trailing behind the rocket. Once the rope was secured onboard the marooned vessel, a steel hawser and a breeches buoy was dragged across from the shore, essentially a cradle and harness which would be used to pull the men to the safe reaches of solid land.

Further on is the harbour: 'The harbour of Port Erroll is a tiny haven of refuge won from the jagged rocks that bound the eastern side of Cruden Bay,' wrote Bram Stoker. 'It is sheltered on the northern side by the cliff which runs as far as the Watter's Mou' and separated from the mouth of the Water of Cruden, with its waste of shifting sands by a high wall of concrete. The harbour faces east, and its first basin is the smaller of the two, the larger opening sharply to the left a little way in. At the best of times, it is not an easy matter to gain the harbour, for only when the tide has fairly risen is it available at all, and the rapid tide which runs up from the Scaurs makes in itself a difficulty at such times.'

The drying green for the fishing nets can be seen on the right-hand side. The original wooden poles that the nets were hung from still survive. A few old fishing boats can also be seen in the harbour area.

Now return to the Kilmarnock Arms Hotel, altogether a round trip of about a mile.

Walk Two: Kilmarnock Arms Hotel to Slains Castle (walking distance: two miles)

This walk starts outside the Kilmarnock Arms Hotel. A word of warning – part of the walk skirts the cliff tops, please keep to the main path. The walk is unsuitable for young children and dogs should be kept on a leash at all times.

Cross the road and walk to the end of Main Street where you will see the Port Erroll Congregational Church on your right hand-side. It's curious that Bram doesn't mention any of the three local churches in his Cruden Bay novels. The following excerpt from *The Mystery of the Sea* suggests there may have been some tension here:

'Doubtless I could have found out all I wanted from some of the ministers of the various houses of religion which hold in Cruden; but I was not wishful to make public, even so far, the mystery which was closing around me. My feeling was partly a saving sense of humour, or the fear of ridicule, and partly a genuine repugnance to enter upon the subject with any one who might not take it as seriously as I could wish.'

Repugnance – ouch! One can guess what happened here. I can only imagine that the local ministers would not have approved of the devilish themes and popish practices set out in *Dracula* …

From the congregational church, take the sign-posted path to Slains Castle via the car park and the woods. Once through the trees you will emerge on the left hand-side of a ravine carved into the local red granite. This formed when the glaciers melted at the end of the Ice Age and huge torrents of water cascaded to the sea by any means possible. All that remains now is a small stream called the Back Burn which seems far too small for the gorge it sits in.

At its sea end the stream takes a dogleg southwards through a deeply-incised channel. This is the Watter's Mou' (The Water's Mouth) and it provides the title for one of Bram Stoker's novels.

Bram Stoker describes it thus:

'It's a natural cleft – formed by primeval fire or earthquake or some sort of natural convulsion – which runs through the vast mass of red granite which forms a promontory running due south. Water has done its work as well as fire in the formation of the gully as it is now, for the drip and flow and rush of water that mark the seasons for countless ages have completed the work of the pristine fire. As one sees this natural mouth of the stream in the rocky face of the cliff, it is hard to realise that nature alone has done the work.'

The excerpt resonates with Van Helsing's description of the location of Dracula's Castle in *Dracula*, as published two years after *The Watter's Mou'* came out.

'The very place, where he have been alive, Un-Dead for all these centuries, is full of strangeness of the geologic and chemical world. There are deep caverns and fissures that reach none know whither. There have been volcanoes, some of whose openings still send out waters of strange properties, and gases that kill or make to vivify.'

This is a theme which runs through Bram Stoker's gothic novels: where evidence for a geological upheaval is found it appears to signify a hotspot of supernatural activity.

The Watter's Mou' is based in Port Erroll and this part of the coast. It's a smuggling tale which revolves around the conflict imposed by circumstance on local coastguard Sailor Willie and his fiancée Maggie McWhirter. Sailor Willie has been asked to look out for a smuggling operation which the authorities believe is about to happen. He discovers that his fiancée's father is involved and when Maggie hints that he should turn a blind eye to the operation; Sailor Willie's strong sense of duty to his job prevents him from doing so. Maggie, who is also steeped in the all-powerful Victorian sense of duty, has only one option left – to sail out from the Watter's Mou' to warn her father that he will be apprehended when he arrives at Port Erroll harbour with the smuggled goods. It will be a highly dangerous undertaking – a storm is brewing up

Sailor Willie, guessing Maggie's intention, points out how hazardous the Watter's Mou' can be for a boat during a storm:

'To try and get in there in this wind would be to court sudden death. Why, lass, it would take a man all he knew just to get out from there, let alone get in, in this weather! And then the chances would be ten to one that he'd be dashed to pieces on the rocks beyond.'

Willie 'pointed to where a line of sharp rocks rose between the billows on the south side of the inlet. Truly, it was a fearful-looking place to be dashed on, for the great waves broke on the rocks with a loud roaring, and even in the semi-darkness they could see the white lines as the waters poured down to leeward in the wake of the heaving wave. The white cluster of rocks looked like a ghostly mouth opened to swallow whatever might come in touch.'

The entrance to the inlet does indeed resemble a mouth. At high tide sharp pyramids of granite rock rise just above the sea at the entrance on the southern side of the inlet. There are about ten 'teeth' altogether, similar in size, and evenly set. The waves surge out revealing the rocks and then surge in covering them again. It creates the impression of a gnashing pair of teeth at the southern entrance of the Watter's Mou'.

Inevitable disaster ensues. Maggie takes a rowing boat out from the Watter's Mou' and makes contact with her father on his boat. She returns to the Watter's Mou' in a raging storm and is ship-wrecked while doing so. Sailor Willie finds her body there, attempts to retrieve it, and is drowned in the process. The book ends on a grim note:

'There, on the very spot whence the boat had set sail on its warning errand, lay its wreckage, and tangled in it the body of the noble girl who had steered it – her brown hair floating wide and twined around the neck of Sailor Willy, who held her tight in his dead arms.

'The requiem of the twain was the roar of the breaking waves and the scream of the white birds that circled round the Watter's Mou'.'

It's a sad end for the two lovers.

On the face of it *The Watter's Mou'* is pure melodrama, yet it reveals a deeper supernatural theme. A journal Bram kept in his younger years, has recently been published together with a commentary provided by the editors, Elizabeth Miller and Dacre Stoker. It's a commonplace book full of anecdotes, jokes, and ideas for stories. Item 41 written in 1881 is the plot for a story with the title *The Angry Waters* – which 'wishes ill to person & kills them then murmurs sorrowfully for ever'. Bram Stoker's handwriting is underneath with the word [Written]. The editors' footnote suggests that this is probably a reference to *The Watter's Mou'*. The implication is that the sea in *The Watter's Mou'* is a supernatural entity prone to powerful emotions. The mouth of the Watter's Mou', with its rocks resembling teeth, has swallowed up the two lovers in a fit of anger, and has left them dead.

This mouth with its sharp teeth is thus linked to a pagan sea spirit. Two years later Count Dracula will be revealed to the world, an undead supernatural monster who also has sharp teeth.

Slains Castle: A short walk takes you to Slains Castle, which is clearly visible up ahead. Slains, with its dramatic cliff-top setting, is popularly said to have inspired *Dracula*. Not quite, as we will see.

But first some practicalities: Slains Castle is a ruin and is not safe to enter. There is an ever-present risk of being hit by falling masonry or taking a tumble on climbing the stairs inside. The cliffs on which it stands are also dangerous. It is common for unguarded dogs to fall off, and accidents have happened to young children here. Be warned.

Slains Castle, as a ruin, looks far more gothic today than it did in Bram Stoker's time. Then it was an oversized mansion lived in by the local aristocrat, the Earl of Erroll. It fell into ruin in the 1920s when the earls ran out of money. A demolition company removed the roof for its lead and slates and sold off parts of the masonry and fittings.

The oldest part of the castle is the tower at the southeast corner built around 1600 or so. Slains Castle isn't the first building of that name. The original castle of medieval age was located four miles down the coast. It was blown up by King James VI in 1594 when the earl took part in a rebellion to reinstate the Catholic faith in Scotland. The earl was exiled for three years, and only allowed to return providing he kept the peace and renounced his Catholic faith.

A substantial addition to the castle was made in the 1820s following the marriage of the 18th earl to the illegitimate daughter of William IV. The earl, having married into royalty, now felt the need to build a royal palace to house his Lady Elizabeth.

The connection between *Dracula* and Slains Castle is nuanced rather than overt. The oft-stated myth that Slains Castle inspired the plot for *Dracula* is wrong. Bram had already planned much of *Dracula* before ever setting foot in Cruden Bay, and this included the castle setting. The castle he had in mind at this point was inspired by drawings he found in books about Transylvania.

Nevertheless, one of the rooms in Slains Castle turns up in Castle Dracula. This is the octagonal room. Here is the description from chapter two of *Dracula*:

'The Count halted, putting down my bags, closed the door, and crossing the room, opened another door which led into a small octagonal room lit by a single lamp, and seemingly without a window of any sort.'

And here's the description of the octagonal room from a 1922 sales document for Slains Castle:

'On the Principal Floor: Entrance Hall (heated with stove) leading to Central Octagonal Interior Hall (heated with stove and lighted from above).'

The octagonal room was used as a waiting room for guests before they were shown into the drawing room to meet the earl. It's plausible that Bram Stoker sat there. There is no direct evidence that Bram was ever inside Slains Castle, although relatives of the earls believe that Bram Stoker was invited in on at least one occasion by the 20th Earl of Erroll.

It's tempting to speculate that the other rooms in Slains Castle were used during the writing phase of the novel. However, there is not an exact correspondence here. The entrance to Castle Dracula was through a ground floor door, whereas Slains Castle was accessed through a door at the top of a flight of steps. One similarity should be noted: Jonathan Harker couldn't find a door knocker or bell at the front door of Castle Dracula; and likewise, no bell or door knocker was provided for the front door of Slains Castle. And also note that the family crest carved in stone above the front door of Slains Castle included the motto, 'Gang Warily' – Go Warily. This would have been good advice for Jonathan Harker in Castle Dracula.

Bram liked to cherry pick the distinctive features he encountered during his travels for use in his novels. The octagonal room in Slains Castle is an example of this. Otherwise, where Slains Castle matters in *Dracula* is that it was usually visible by Bram Stoker while he was writing it. The sight of the castle dramatically perched on the edge of the cliff top undoubtedly acted as a stimulus to Bram's imagination as he put the words together.

For the record here are the instances, apart from *Dracula,* where Slains Castle has appeared in actual or disguised form in Bram's novels. It obviously made a huge impression on him:

The Watter's Mou':
'… on one side a steep grassy slope leads towards the new castle of Slains, and on the other rises a sheer bank, with tufts of the thick grass growing on the ledges, where the earth has been blown.'

The Mystery of the Sea:
'My own section for watching was between Slains Castle and Dunbuy, as wild and rocky a bit of coast as any one could wish to see. Behind Slains runs in a long narrow inlet with beetling cliffs, sheer on either side, and at its entrance a wild turmoil of rocks are hurled together in titanic confusion.'

The Man:
Slains Castle doubles up as Castle Lannoy:

'Lannoy was on the north-eastern coast, the castle standing at the base of a wide promontory stretching far into the North Sea … No habitation other than an isolated fisher's cottage was to be seen between the little fishing-port at the northern curve away to the south, where beyond a waste of sandhills and strand another tiny fishing-village nestled under a high cliff, sheltering it from northerly wind.'

If the similarity to Cruden Bay isn't made clear enough, Lannoy also has a dangerous reef of rocks called the Skyres similar to the Skares near Cruden Bay.

The Jewel of Seven Stars:
Kyllion House appears to be modelled on Slains Castle:

'A great grey stone mansion of the Jacobean period; vast and spacious, standing high over the sea on the very verge of a high cliff. When we had swept round the curve of the avenue cut through the rock, and come out on the high plateau on which the house stood, the crash and murmur of waves breaking against rock far below us came with an invigorating breath of moist sea air.'

The ancient spirit of an Egyptian mummy was brought to life at Kyllion, a circumstance inspiring a number of Hollywood films. As an in joke, Bram Stoker named Kyllion after the editor of *Dracula*, Otto Kyllmann.

From Slains castle, return the way you came, or alternatively, for the energetic, walk up the coast for about a mile to the spectacular arch of Dunbuy. To reach Dunbuy, walk westwards along the path leading to the car park on the main road. Pass by a deep narrow gorge and the cliff-top path runs along the western side of the gorge. You will need to step up on the low-lying wall to access the path. It's a spectacular walk, taken many a time by Bram Stoker, but do keep to the path – the cliffs are dangerous.

Walk Three: Kilmarnock Arms Hotel to Whinnyfold (five miles round trip)

Practicalities – wear walking shoes or boots. The walk along the beach is easy enough, although you will cross three shallow streams on the way. At the far end, a bit of a scramble is involved on ascending the path to Whinnyfold. It can be muddy following wet weather, so watch where you step. It is possible to sink ankle-deep into the mud in places.

From the Kilmarnock Arms Hotel walk down Main Street and then onto Harbour Street. On the right-hand side is the Lady's Bridge which takes you over the Cruden Water onto the beach. The Lady's Bridge is named after the women of the village who collected money to have the original bridge built in 1923. It was rebuilt in 2016.

Cruden Bay beach is a wide sandy beach, one and a half miles long, which lies between two rocky promontories. Its broad curve is backed by sand dunes covered in lime-green marram grass. Two-thirds of the way along can be seen the prominent hill of the Hawklaw rising above the dunes.

Here's how Bram saw this view: 'If Cruden Bay is to be taken figuratively as a mouth, with the sand hills for soft palate, and the green Hawklaw as the tongue, the rocks which work the extremities are its teeth.'

Not many would see Cruden Bay beach as a mouth with teeth, although Bram Stoker did. Later in the novel from which this excerpt is taken, *The Mystery of the Sea*, he writes about 'fang-like rocks rising out of the deep water'. The resonance with *Dracula* is deliberate; it was while walking along the beach or sitting on the rocks at the far end that he thought through the writing phase of his famous novel.

Bram would take a walk along the beach at 7am every morning before returning for breakfast. Mrs Cruickshank, who worked at the Port Erroll Post Office, recalled that Bram dressed in tweeds with a round beret on his head. 'He became a familiar figure with his stout walking-stick as he strolled along the sands and the cliffs,' she said. Another resident remembers him wearing a long cape and a wide-brimmed hat. His pose was highly distinctive; Bram Stoker walked along the beach with his hands behind his back, head down with a slight stoop, and looked as if he was utterly absorbed in intense thought. A rapid walker, his morning trips took him along the beach to the tiny fishing village of Whinnyfold and back again.

A sense of how he marvelled at the nature around him comes from *The Mystery of the Sea*. Bram keeps repeating variations on the first line of a psalm throughout the book. He probably sang it as he walked along the Cruden Bay shoreline:

> Heaven and earth, and sea and air,
> All their Maker's praise declare;
> Wake, my soul, awake and sing:
> Now thy grateful praises bring.
>
> See the glorious orb of day
> Breaking through the clouds his way;
> Moon and stars with silvery light
> Praise Him through the silent night.
>
> See how He hath everywhere
> Made this earth so rich and fair;
> Hill and vale and fruitful land,
> All things living, show His hand.

On other occasions he walked along the beach with his wife Florence. This probably inspired the following, where the main character is on Cruden Bay beach at twilight with his fiancée:

'The spirits of my companion and myself yielded to this silent influence of the coming night. Unconsciously we walked close together and in step; and were silent, wrapt in the beauty around us. To me it was a gentle ecstasy. To be alone with her in such a way, in such a place, was the good of all heaven and all earth in one. And so for many minutes we went slowly on our way along the deserted sand, and in hearing of the music of the sounding sea and the echoing shore.'

That last phrase sums up the experience of walking along Cruden Bay beach – one does indeed hear *'the music of the sounding sea and the echoing shore'*.

Shallow streams cross the beach and are normally easy enough to cross. The first of these, the one closest to the village, is known locally as the Bleedy Burn. The name is age-old and recalls the memory of a battle between the Vikings and the Scots army said to have taken place in 1012. The battle raged over the sand dunes behind the beach and on the land which now forms the golf course. The stream is said to have ran red with blood for three days after the battle; and as such would have made a stark contrast with the flesh-coloured sand as it trickled over the beach …

A feature to look out for on Cruden Bay beach are the sand devils which appear when gusts of wind blow the dry sand along the foreshore. As the sand grains speed along and writhe for a second or two they resemble ghostly serpents. Once the wind dies down, the lighter sand settles over the underlying darker wet sand to form patterns which resemble the outlines of dancing ghosts. Perhaps a similar sight inspired the famous scenes in *Dracula*, when the three vampire sisters appeared before Jonathan Harker:

'Something made me start up, a low, piteous howling of dogs somewhere far below in the valley, which was hidden from my sight. Louder it seemed to ring in my ears, and the floating moats of dust to take new shapes to the sound as they danced in the moonlight … Quicker and quicker danced the dust. The moonbeams seemed to quiver as they went by me into the mass of gloom beyond. More and more they gathered till they seemed to take dim phantom shapes … The phantom shapes, which were becoming gradually materialised from the moonbeams, were those three ghostly women to whom I was doomed.'

The Sand Craigs: At the southern end of the beach are a number of rocky crags which Bram Stoker refers to as the Sand Craigs. The nearest is accessible at low to medium tide (be warned: it becomes an island at high tide). It's a grassy knoll with a stone cairn on its summit. This was probably one of Bram's favourite spots in Cruden Bay. Here's how he describes it in his short story 'Crooken Sands' – the main character Mr Markam is on holiday in Cruden Bay and has taken a late evening walk:

'The tide was out and the beach firm as a rock, so he strolled southwards to nearly the end of the bay. Here he was attracted by two isolated rocks some little way out from the edge of the dunes, so he strolled towards them. When he reached the nearest one, he climbed it, and, sitting there elevated some fifteen or twenty feet over the waste of sand enjoyed the lovely, peaceful prospect.'

First published in 1894, and the year of Bram's second visit to Cruden Bay, the tale hints why the author returned there year after year:

'For a good while Mr Markam sat and looked at the rising moon and the growing area of light which followed its rise. Then he turned and faced eastwards and sat with his chin in his hand looking seawards and revelling in the peace and beauty and freedom of the scene. The roar of London – the darkness and the strife and weariness of London life seemed to have passed quite away, and he lived at the moment a freer and higher life.'

The view is spectacular: 'The full moon was behind him, and its light lit up the bay so that its fringe of foam, the dark outline of the headland, and the stakes of the salmon-nets were all emphasised.' He could see in 'the brilliant yellow glow' the lights in the windows of Port Erroll and 'those of the distant castle of the laird trembled like stars through the sky'. It made a lasting impression: 'For a long time he sat and drank in the beauty of the scene, and his soul seemed to feel a peace that it had not known for many days.'

You can look out from the Sand Craigs today and see this view more or less exactly as written. The lights of 'the distant castle of the laird' were those of Slains Castle. The only difference is that Slains Castle is now a ruin, whereas it had been inhabited in Bram Stoker's time.

A newspaper interview given by Florence Stoker suggests that this spot was where Bram spent hours mulling over the writing of *Dracula*. Florence told the reporter in 1927:

'When he was at work on Dracula, we were all frightened of

him. It was up on a lonely part of the east coast of Scotland, and he seemed to get obsessed by the spirit of the thing. There he would sit for hours, like a great bat, perched on the rocks of the shore, or wander alone up and down the sandhills thinking it out.'

Bram was edgy while writing *Dracula* at Cruden Bay and Florence and Noel were disturbed by his behaviour. They found him distant and prone to an outburst of temper if interrupted while writing or thinking about the novel. It's possible that Bram may have been using the method acting techniques of Henry Irving to get into the mind of its characters. If so, he must have presented a fiercesome sight as he marched up and down the beach in the embodiment of Jonathan Harker or Count Dracula!

Sometime later Florence was asked to make a contribution to a booklet of recipes published in 1912 by the Cruden Parish Church. The booklet *Cruden Recipes and Wrinkles* was printed as a souvenir for a bazaar to be held in the church grounds to raise money for renovation of the church. The recipes had been contributed by the congregation and friends. In amongst them are the 'wrinkles' – pithy phrases of wisdom and advice. One of the two recipes contributed by Florence Stoker was 'The "Dracula" Salad':

'Arrange alternative slices of ripe tomatoes and ripe purple egg shaped plums in dish and dress with oil and vinegar French Dressing'

From the Sand Craigs, take the rough path to Whinnyfold. The path is accessed by walking along the stony part of the beach and then through a gate on the shore. Take care on walking up the slope here as the ground can get boggy. A path takes you around the headland to Whinnyfold. On the way you will pass by the site of a seal colony on rocks near the waterline. They are not used to humans, although you will not scare them. Curiosity will take hold – they will jump off the rocks and swim towards you to get a better look.

Pass by a rocky beach called Broadhaven with its distinctive rock arch called 'The Puir Mon' [The Poor Man]. Bram described the rock, 'through whose base, time and weather have worn a hole through which one may walk dryshod'.

Reach the headland from which you can catch sight of both the houses of Whinnyfold and the reefs of the Skares. This is the spot where the hero of *The Mystery of the Sea* builds his home. It's also I suspect the spot where Bram Stoker would have built a retirement home if he had made his fortune from the sales of *Dracula* (which he didn't).

One of the locals said that Bram would spend hours on this spot looking over the deadly reefs of The Skares. Here's Bram's description of the reefs:

'For half a mile or more the rocks rise through the sea singly or in broken masses ending in a dangerous cluster known as "The Skares" and which has had for centuries its full toll of wreck and disaster. Did the sea hold its dead where they fell, its floor around The Skares would be whitened with their bones, and new islands could build themselves with the piling wreckage.'

There have been so many shipwrecks on the Skares down the centuries, and the seabed is undoubtedly littered with wreckage and the remains of the drowned sailors. Perhaps Bram was hyper-sensitive to the mood of a place and would have deeply empathised with the fate of these lost souls as he stood on the cliffs.

The Skares is an area of geological disturbance as is the Watter's Mou' and Bram's fictional Castle Dracula which is situated on an old volcano. The local granite, once molten magma, had thrust upwards through the solid rock at its margins. The boundary between the two rocks is visible at the northern edge of the pebbly beach of Broadhaven:

'That union must have been originally a wild one; there are evidences of an upheaval which must have shaken the earth to its centre. Here and there are great masses of either species of rock hurled upwards in every conceivable variety of form ...'

Whinnyfold and Crookit Lum Cottage: Walk into the hamlet of Whinnyfold with its dense cluster of 24 houses lying almost flush with the cliff top. Note that if you visit the village by car it is difficult to park here.

Whinnyfold had been a fishing village in Bram Stoker's time.

Bram spent the summer of 1910 in residence at Crookit Lum cottage (at the far end of the main street). He is only known to have stayed there once. Today the Crookit Lum is a private residence – please respect the privacy of the residents and don't disturb them. It's a two storey-house with gabled windows and a small extension which was once the washhouse. The chimney leans slightly into the street, hence the name of the cottage in the local dialect which means 'crooked chimney'.

Bram's landlady at The Crookit Lum was Isy Cay (pronounced Isee Kigh), who lived with her aging mother Jane. One of the locals recalls her mother telling her that Isy Cay ran a teashop in the Crookit Lum, and Bram and Florence would often stop off for tea and scones on their walks from Cruden Bay. Only later did they stay in the cottage. Isy and her mother moved into the washhouse, the northern end of the house and the part with the crooked chimney. The rooms in the rest of the cottage were rented out.

Bram Stoker was ailing badly on his last visit in 1910; he suffered from kidney disease and had suffered a stroke a few years previously. Mrs Cruickshank from the post office came to visit him at the Crookit Lum: 'It was plain to see he was very ill'. Local resident, George Hay, mentions how Bram Stoker would lie in a hammock for hours at a time staring at The Skares. On other occasions he would rise up and go for a walk along Cruden Bay beach, 'the tall, bearded Irishman, his cloak flying in the wind tamping about the heavy sand, prodding it with the heavy stick, waving his arm and shouting at the great rollers as they thundered up the beach, and altogether behaving in such an outlandish way that George's second cousin, Eliza, who worked at the Kilmarnock Arms, was afraid to walk home across the sands to Whinnyfold, and took the long way round'. These observations tie in with a comment by his biographer and a relative of Bram Stoker, Daniel Farson, who was told by his mother that by this stage he was 'rather dotty.' When Farson queried this, she replied, 'Well, really very dotty.'

Despite his illness, he managed to find the energy to work. According to his biographer Harry Ludlam, Bram's publishers had asked for a new thriller, and he started writing *The Lair of the White Worm* while at Whinnyfold.

Near the Crookit Lum cottage is a path down to the shore: 'a steep zigzag path running down to the stony beach far below where the fishers keep their boats and which is protected from almost the wildest seas by the great black rock — the Caudman, — which fills the middle of the little bay, leaving deep channels on either hand.'

A walk down takes you to the pebbly shore where the fishermen left their boats. Look northwards and you can see the entrance to the cave where the Spanish treasure was found in *The Mystery of the Sea*. To the right of the cave entrance can be seen Lord Nelson's Rock. Mentioned by Bram Stoker, it's said to resemble the famous admiral in profile.

A dramatic scene in *The Mystery of the Sea* ensues here. A procession of ghosts of the sailors drowned at the Skares emerges from the sea:

'Up the steep path came a silent procession of ghostly figures, so misty of outline that through the grey green of their phantom being the rocks and moonlit sea were apparent, and even the velvet blackness of the shadows of the rocks did not lose their gloom. And yet each figure was defined so accurately that every feature, every particle of dress or accoutrement could be discerned. Even the sparkle of their eyes in that grim waste of ghostly grey was like the lambent flashes of phosphoric light in the foam of moving water cleft by a swift prow. There was no need for me to judge by the historical sequence of their attire, or by any inference of hearing; I knew in my heart that these were the ghosts of the dead who had been drowned in the waters of the Cruden Skares.

Indeed, the moments of their passing — and they were many for the line was of sickening length — became to me a lesson of the long flight of time. At the first were skin-clad savages with long, wild hair matted, then others with rude, primitive clothing. And so on in historic order men, aye, and here and there a woman, too, of many lands, whose garments were of varied cut and substance. Red-haired Vikings and black-haired Celts and Phoenicians, fair-haired Saxons and swarthy Moors in flowing robes. At first the figures, chiefly of the barbarians, were not many; but as the sad procession passed along, I could see how each later year had brought its ever growing tale of loss and disaster, and added more and faster to the grim harvest of the sea.'

After walking up the zigzag path, the ghosts make a procession along the cliff tops to Cruden Bay beach. They then turn inland towards the sand dunes, their destination – St Olaf's well. Here they disappear back into the earth. The well was once a holy well where pilgrims would drink water to cure their disease. It's now surrounded by Cruden Bay golf course, and a traditional wooden well feature marks its location.

The march of the ghosts has mistakenly been reported by Bram's biographers as based on local folk lore; not those locals know anything about this. It actually derives from scenes in Walt Whitman's poem *Sleepers*. Bram Stoker was obsessed with the American's poetry.

From Whinnyfold, return back to Cruden Bay the way you came retracing in part the procession of the ghosts!

Miscellaneous

This section deals with localities associated with Bram Stoker which do not fit neatly into the three walks. Two of these are located on Aulton Road, which is the main road leading south from the bridge next to the Kilmarnock Arms hotel.

About 50 yards beyond the bridge on the left-hand side is the Aulton Garage which is located in an old grain store. Bram used the building as the location for the wedding in *The Watter's Mou'*. The scene in the novel was inspired by a village bazaar held in the grain store in 1894 to raise money to build the village hall. Bram was there with Florence and his son Noel.

A bit further along and opposite the St Olaf Hotel is the entrance to Station Road which led to Cruden Bay Railway Station, now demolished. It was built in 1897 and used by Bram *en route* to and from his London home. Before the line was built, he took the train north to the nearby town of Ellon and from there a pony and trap to Cruden Bay. It's curious that these travel arrangements resemble the journey taken by Jonathan Harker to Castle Dracula in Transylvania!

On the left-hand side of Aulton Road is the entrance to Cruden Bay Golf Course where the magnificent Cruden Bay hotel was opened in 1899 as a luxury destination for the upper class. The hotel was demolished in the 1950s. Bram never stayed there as far I know, and he isn't known to have played golf on the course either. His wife Florence was a keen golfer and was said to have been the prettiest woman ever to have graced the fairways.

One other locality outside Cruden Bay was visited by Bram Stoker. About a mile north of the village is the coastal feature known as the Bullers of Buchan. Stop off at the car park and walk along the path through a small group of houses. A short distance to the north along the cliff path takes you to the Bullers (a dangerous spot for children and dogs). Here you look directly down at a collapsed sea cave where the narrow entrance arch has remained intact. During a storm the sea below 'boils' when the waves rush in through the arch.

BRAM STOKER AND WHITBY

Bram Stoker's Summer Holiday in Whitby, 1890

Having been to the ancient seaport of Whitby myself on several occasions, I have a good sense of what Bram found so appealing about the small fishing and vacation town in Yorkshire. Firstly, for Bram, it was a long way – both geographically and emotionally, from London. Bram probably felt some relief escaping London for a holiday in Whitby; similar to escaping the pressures of Dublin by going to Clontarf and the beach at Greystones. Each of these towns provided a relaxing escape for Bram away from the hustle and bustle of the big city. Secondly, water dominates the scenery in Whitby as it does in Greystones. Bram was born within view of the bay in Clontarf; throughout his life he was drawn back to the sea: Greystones, Whitby, Cruden Bay; and was comfortable crossing the Atlantic more than twenty times. Bram's own experiences on and near the water, his near mystical love of the sea gave him comfort and allowed his sense of imagination and creativity to flourish.

Even today, the atmosphere in Whitby is perfectly suited for a horror novel. Many of the very well-known and identifiable locations in Whitby appear in *Dracula* just as Bram saw them, and not much differently than they appear today. By day the town seems idyllic yet alluring: narrow cobblestone streets wind their way on either side of the Esk River; on the West Cliff a massive whalebone arch (currently the third replica (2003) of the original jawbone which was erected c.1853 and which is now in the Whitby Archives and Heritage Centre) straddles the walkway. However, in the evening when the sun goes down, the sea mist rolls in and as a cold chill permeates everything, one can feel an involuntary shudder as the town is transformed into a dark and sinister scene. And day or night, iconic Whitby Abbey, perched high on East Cliff at the top of the 199 steps, next door to St Mary's Church and graveyard, adds to the general sense of the Gothic.

There is no question that Bram's one vacation in Whitby in the summer of 1890 made a major impact on his writing *Dracula*. As the pages of Bram's notes for *Dracula* are not all dated, it is not possible to know precisely when and where all of his ideas were generated. But significant revisions were made as a result of Bram's visit to Whitby – notes made before his providential holiday in Whitby indicate Bram's vampire was named 'Count Wampyr' and the count would arrive in England via the port of Dover. Obviously the atmosphere in Whitby, the physical setting and the town's layers of history and local legends suited Bram's purpose perfectly. And one particular book by William Wilkinson (*An Account of the Principalities of Wallachia and Moldoviu* (1820)) that Bram borrowed from the Whitby Subscription Library provided him with a lesson in Wallachian history and the inspiration to change the name of his vampire Count from Wampyr to Count Dracula.

In 1890, Bram, his wife, Florence and son, Noel stayed in Mrs Veazey's guesthouse, at 6 Royal Crescent – the same Crescent where Mina and Lucy spend their fictional vacation. Today, fans of the novel can follow a modern-day *Dracula* trail and retrace the cross-town, late night walk that brought Mina from the West Cliff, across the famous swing bridge over the River Esk and along the cobblestone streets, up the 199 steps into St Mary's Church graveyard where she found Lucy lying on a grave after her encounter with Count Dracula. The Great Northern Railway line that the carried the Stokers back to London from Whitby also transported the fifty boxes of mysterious dirt to different locations in London.

When Bram travelled, he made a habit of getting to know the locals who could tell him a town's stories – in Whitby he sought out the coastguard and rescue crews. He managed to befriend William Petherick, a commissioned boatman whom Bram convinced to give him a page from the logbook of the Coast Guard Station entitled 'Details of Wrecks at Whitby'. This page, found in Bram's notes, includes the strange circumstances of the wreck of the *Dimitry*, a Russian schooner, which ran aground in a storm in 1885. In typical fashion Bram co-opted this wreck and the schooner, ballasted with silver sand (which landed under full sail on Tate Hill Sands during a very strong storm), became the *Demeter* bringing Count Dracula to Whitby.

One hundred and twenty five years since *Dracula* was published, it is impossible to image the novel without Whitby, and difficult to imagine Whitby without *Dracula*. The historical Whitby and the Whitby in *Dracula* seem to exist in a mutually beneficial, symbiotic relationship, with Whitby as a very special, living time capsule – immediately recognisable as Bram described it.

THE BRAM STOKER COLLECTION

It gives me great pleasure to help publicise the acquisition of the John Moore Collection by Emory University's Stuart A Rose Library in Atlanta, Georgia, and to encourage researchers to avail themselves of this great treasure.

I have spent the last thirteen years in my quest to understand Bram Stoker and the research that went into writing *Dracula*. During that time, John Moore of Dublin, Ircland generously shared his unparalleled Bram Stoker-*Dracula* library with me (and other researchers). Flying to Dublin for research is always time consuming and expensive, but enjoying stimulating conversation with John in Buswell's or soaking up his enthusiasm as he described his latest Stoker acquisition has always been a priceless experience. John and I forged a friendship, based on our common desire to learn all that we can about Bram Stoker, and to share what we learn with others. John's collection has long been considered the most complete Stoker collection in existence, and the Rose Library is to be commended for helping John accomplish his dream that it stay intact.

Now, this incomparable collection of everything Stoker and *Dracula* is at home in Emory's Rose Library, only a two and a half hour drive from my home – and fortunately for those who live further away, it will be digitised in due course. I will take advantage of my close proximity to Atlanta and continue my research, while I give thanks to John for his 40 years of Stoker stewardship, and to the Rose Library for providing a most suitable home.

The following is a condensed version of the information about the Stoker Papers of the John Moore Collection taken directly from the Rose Library website.

https://findingaids.library.emory.edu/documents/moore1514/

Stuart A Rose Manuscript, Archives, and Rare Book Library Atlanta, GA 30322, rose.library@emory.edu

Creator: Moore, John (John Francis), 1942, August 6-, collector
Title: John Moore Bram Stoker collection, 1707-2018 [bulk 1878-1980]
Call Number: Manuscript Collection No. 1514
Extent: 11.75 linear feet (18 boxes), 3 oversized papers boxes and 5 oversized papers folders (OP) 5 bound volumes (BV), 1 oversized bound volume (OBV), and 16 extra-oversized papers XOP
Abstract: Collection of materials, accumulated by John Moore, documenting the life and work of Bram Stoker, including primarily letters, photographs, printed material, and memorabilia.
Language: Materials entirely in English.

Administrative Information

Restrictions on Access
Special restrictions apply: All audiovisual material in this collection is commercial and cannot be digitised or otherwise reproduced due to copyright law. Researchers are welcome to request audiovisual items to examine their packaging.

Researchers must contact the Rose Library in advance for access to unprocessed born digital materials in this collection. Collection restrictions, copyright limitations, or technical complications may hinder the Rose Library's ability to provide access to unprocessed born digital materials.

Related Materials in Other Repositories
Papers of the Stoker Family, Manuscripts and Archives, the Library of Trinity College (Dublin, Ireland)

Separated Material
The Rose Library holds books collected by John Moore. These materials may be located in the Emory University online catalog by searching for: Moore, John (John Francis), 1942 August 6-, collector.

Source
Purchased from Kennys Bookshop and Art Galleries, LTD., representing John Moore, 2020

Custodial History

The materials in this collection were amassed by John Moore from a variety of disparate sources, including rare book and manuscript dealers. Provenance for much of the collection is unknown. Kennys staff packed and shipped the collection to Rose Library

Collection Description

Biographical Note

Bram Stoker was born in Dublin, Ireland in 1847 to Abraham Stoker and Charlotte Thornley Stoker. He was one of seven children. He attended Trinity College, Dublin. He married Florence Balcomb in 1878 and the couple had one child, Irving Noel Thornley Stoker. Following his graduation from Trinity, Stoker worked in the Irish Civil Service and as the theatre critic for the *Dublin Evening Mail*. It was in this capacity that he met and became friends with English Shakespearean actor Henry Irving, eventually moving his family to London and becoming business manager of Irving's Lyceum Theatre. Stoker published the gothic horror novel *Dracula* in 1897.

John Moore is a former business consultant and spent much of his life acquiring book and manuscript materials documenting the life of Bram Stoker, his works, and the enduring legacy of the *Dracula* story in particular.

Scope and Content Note

The collection consists of material acquired by John Moore documenting the life and works of Bram Stoker from 1707-2013. It includes letters; Bram Stoker writings and Lyceum Theatre business records; photographs, artwork, and audiovisual material; printed material; memorabilia; *Dracula* derivatives and Stoker scholarship; and papers of John Moore documenting his collecting activities. Letters in the collection contain missives from Stoker; his wife, Florence; his brother, Tom; his close friend, Hall Caine; Lyceum Theatre actors, Henry Irving and Ellen Terry; and other members of Stoker's social and professional circles. There is no true correspondence in this collection and letters do not document any back-and-forth communication. Bram Stoker writings and Lyceum Theatre business records include typescripts of writings by Stoker as well as a ledger of returns from a run of *Othello* at the Lyceum Theatre in 1881.

Photographs depict Stoker, Irving, Terry, and Cain, as well as numerous Stoker family members. Artwork includes sketches and paintings depicting Stoker and Irving, as well as four original works by Pamela Colman Smith, including one that may depict Ellen Terry, and original costume designs for an unidentified production of *Dracula*. Printed material includes numerous playbills and programs for theatrical adaptations of *Dracula* and productions of plays at the Lyceum Theatre (London, England) starring Irvin and Terry. There are also numerous film posters, lobby cards, and press books promoting film adaptations of *Dracula* and subsequent films featuring the Dracula character, as well as other Hammer (England) and Universal (United States) horror films. Memorabilia consists primarily of dolls, mugs, figurines, and toys depicting Dracula. *Dracula* derivatives and Stoker scholarship contains scripts and screenplays for film adaptations of Stoker's novel *Dracula* and subsequent films featuring the Dracula character.

Audiovisual material consists of video recordings of *Dracula* other horror films as well as a recording of an Irish television program featuring Stoker material.

Arrangement Note
Organized into 9 series: (1) Letters, (2) Bram Stoker writings and Lyceum Theatre business records, (3) Photographs, (4) Artwork, (5) Printed material, (6) Memorabilia, (7) Dracula derivatives and Stoker scholarship, (8) Audiovisual material, and (9) John Moore papers

Series 1 – Letters, 1707-2010 [bulk 1878-1923], Boxes 1 – 2 and OP 1
Scope and Content Note
The series consists of letters written or received by Bram Stoker, family members, friends, and colleagues, including his wife, Florence; his brother, Tom; his close friend, Hall Caine; Lyceum Theatre actors, Henry Irving and Ellen Terry. There is no true correspondence in this collection and letters do not document any back-and-forth communication. Many of Irving's letters were penned by Stoker and signed by Irving, documenting Stoker's role as business manager of the Lyceum Theatre. Numerous letters of both Stoker and Irving appear on letterhead from Irving's various tours of the United States, during which Stoker accompanied him as manager. The series contains a significant number of letters from Tom Stoker to his wife Enid,

documenting both their romantic relationship and his work and travels as a member of the British civil service in India.

Series 2 – Bram Stoker writings and Lyceum Theatre business records, circa 1871-1911 Boxes 2 – 3 and OBV 1
Scope and Content Note

The series consists of writings by Bram Stoker and Lyceum Theatre business records from circa 1871-1911. Stoker's writings are typescripts of articles and short stories, including the unpublished 'The Russian Professor'. The business records of the Lyceum Theatre are primarily a single ledger book documenting returns from a run of *Othello* in 1881. The ledger was kept by Stoker as business manager of the theatre.

Series 3 – Photographs, 1866-2013 [bulk 1866-1928], Boxes 3 – 4, OP 1, and BV 1
Scope and Content Note

The series consists of photographs, artwork, and one audiovisual item. Photographs are primarily of identified and unidentified members of the extended Stoker family. There are also photographs of Henry Irving and Ellen Terry, including portraits of them in costume. Many of Terry's photographs are autographed.

Series 4 – Artwork, circa 1873-1924, Boxes 4 – 5 and OP 1
Scope and Content Note

The series consists of original artwork from circa 1873-1924, including a pen and ink sketch of Bram Stoker by an unknown artist, works by Pamela Colman Smith, drawings and a painting of Henry Irving, and a drawing of Hall Caine. One of the works by Pamela Colman Smith is a watercolour and pencil drawing of a woman on stage, which may be Ellen Terry. There is also a partial set of costume designs from an unidentified production of *Dracula*, including sketches for Wilhelmina (Mina; labeled as Willy on the sketch) Murray; Jonathan Harker; Arthur Holmwood, Lord Godalming; Dr John Seward; and Renfield.

Series 5 – Printed material, circa 1820-2016, Boxes 5 – 10 and 18, OP 1 – 8, XOP 1 – 16, and BV 2 – 5
Scope and Content Note

The series consists of printed material relating to Bram Stoker, Henry Irving, Ellen Terry, the Lyceum Theatre (London, England), Stoker's novel *Dracula*, and the artistic and pop culture legacy of the novel. The series contains numerous playbills and programs for theatre productions, including Shakespearean plays performed at the Lyceum Theatre by Irving and Terry; mid-century productions of *Dracula* the play; and productions of other plays about vampires, both those produced prior to the novel *Dracula*'s publication and after the novel was adapted for the theatre. There are also film posters for the many film adaptations of the novel, film sequels, other vampire movies, and other horror films, particularly monster movies produced by Hammer Films (England) and Universal (United States). The series contains lobby cards and pressbooks for many of the films as well. Stamps depicting *Dracula* books and films, predominantly from the United States, United Kingdom, and Ireland, comprise another significant portion of the series.

Series 6 – Memorabilia, circa 1905-2018, Boxes 10-11 and 13 – 17
Scope and Content Note
The series consists of memorabilia relating to Bram Stoker and his novel *Dracula*, including dolls, mugs, toys, and figurines. The series also contains collectible film cells from *Dracula* and other vampire movies.

Series 7 – *Dracula* derivatives and Stoker scholarship, 1945-2002, Boxes 11 – 12 and OP 1
Scope and Content Note
The series consists of *Dracula* derivatives and scholarship about Bram Stoker. The majority of the items in the series are scripts and screenplays for adaptations of Stoker's novel *Dracula* and subsequent films about the character.

Series 8 – Audiovisual material, 1931-2021, Box 18
Scope and Content Note
The series consists primarily of video recordings of film adaptations of Bram Stoker's novel *Dracula* and subsequent movies about the Dracula character. There is also one audiobook of the novel *Dracula* and a recording of an Irish television program featuring Stoker material

Series 9 – John Moore papers, Restrictions on Access
This series is closed for processing

TIMELINE

I've long been fascinated by the events which led to the writing of *Dracula*, as the book is as much a sum of the author's life as it can possibly be. To understand the book, it is necessary to also understand all the many events – some large, some small – which in some way shaped Bram Stoker's life.

The following pages contain the significant details that I see as milestones in Bram's life, childhood, growing up, early work-life … all of course leading to his writing *Dracula*.

I've also included some details of events that took place post *Dracula* in order to complete the picture of his life.

I'm grateful to the talented artist and graphic designer Alistair Hughes for taking my basic list and making it look spectacular!

Bran Castle

A timeline of important events in Bram Stoker's life and legacy

November 8
Abraham Stoker Jr
Born in Clontarf

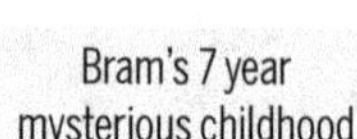

1847

1848

1848-49 Potato Famine
and cholera epidemic
continues in Ireland

1850

The Great Famine ends

Bram's 7 year
mysterious childhood
illness ends (1847-54)

1854

1858

Attends Bective House
College at 15 Rutland
Square, Dublin

Wins prize for drawing
at Royal Dublin Society

1861

Becomes Athletic
Champion at Trinity College

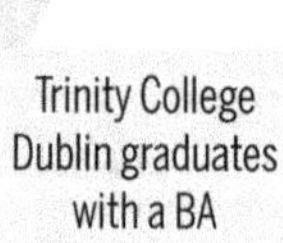

1864

Joins the Civil Service at
Dublin Castle as a Petty
Sessions Clerk

1866

In Marsh's library Bram
does research on religious
conflict and other topics

Trinity College
Dublin graduates
with a BA
(1864-70)

1870

Presents the paper
*Means of Improvement
in Composition*
at Trinity College

Writes theatre reviews for
The Dublin Evening Mail

1871

November 13 *The Necessity
for Political Honesty*, Trinity College
Historical Society; Address delivered
in the Dining Hall of Trinity College

1872

The Crystal Cup published
in London Society Magazine

1873

1873-74 Becomes the editor of
the *Irish Echo* Newspaper

1874

A founding member of
the Dublin Painting and
Sketching Club

*The Primrose Path,
The Chain of Destiny
& Buried Treasure*
published in
The Shamrock Journal

1875

Obtains a MA from
Trinity College

1876

Promoted to Inspector Petty Sessions throughout Ireland

Met Henry Irving in Shelbourne Hotel Dublin

Death of Abraham Stoker Sr in Cava de Tirreni, Italy

1878

Married Florence Balcombe

Moved to London

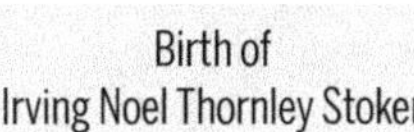

1879

Birth of Irving Noel Thornley Stoker

Duties of Clerks of Petty Sessions published by John Falconer, Dublin. Non Fiction

1882

Under The Sunset, London: Sampson Low, Marston, Searle and Rivington.

Attempted rescue of a suicide victim in Thames river, awarded Bronze medal by The Royal Humane Society

1883

First US Tour for Lyceum Theatre and Henry Irving

1885

A Glimpse of America lecture given in London

1886

The Dualists in the 1887 edition of *The Theatre Annual*

Jack the Ripper Murders in London

1888

Starts doing research on *Dracula* at The London Library

The Snake's Pass, London, Sampson Low, Marston, Searle and Rivington

1890

Bram, Florence and Noel take a three week holiday in Whitby

April 30 called to the English Bar

Walking tour of northern Scotland discovers Cruden Bay, Aberdeenshire

1893-1910 spent 13 summer holidays in Cruden Bay

1895

The Squaw published in *Holly Leaves*, the Christmas number of *The Illustrated Sporting and Dramatic News*, London.

1895

The Watters Mou', London, A. Constable

Invested with Mark Twain on
the Page Compositor

Thornley Stoker and
Henry Irving knighted

Writes large portions of *Dracula* at
Kilmarnock Arms Hotel, Cruden Bay

1895

*The Shoulder
of Shasta*,
London,
A. Constable

Dracula published by
A. Constable, London

1897

Staged reading of
Dracula to protect
dramatic rights copyright

Henry Irving falls
ill with pleurisy

1898

Fire destroys Lyceum sets

Miss Betty, London,
C. A. Pearson

Dracula published in the
US by Doubleday and
McClure, New York

1899

*The Mystery
of the Sea*,
London,
Heinemann

1902

Death of Charlotte Stoker
in Dublin

1903

*The Jewel of the
Seven Stars*, London,
Heinemann, revised
in 1912

Final US tour of Lyceum
Theatre and Henry Irving

1904

The Man (also called
The Gates of Life),
London, Heinemann.

Bram suffers a minor
stroke

1905

Henry Irving dies after
a performance at the
Bradford Theatre

1906

*Personal Reminisces of
Henry Irving* London:
Heinemann, becomes
a best seller

*The World's Greatest
Shipbuilding Yard*
article published

1907

1908

*Snowbound: The Record of
a Theatrical Touring Party*,
London, Collier

The Lady of the Shroud,
London, Heinemann

1909

Lady Athlyne,
London,
Heinemann

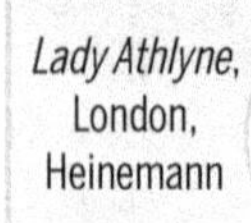

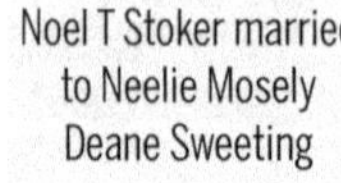

Noel T Stoker married
to Neelie Mosely
Deane Sweeting

1910

Famous Impostors, London, Sidgewick & Jackson

1910

The Lair of the White Worm, London, William Rider

1911

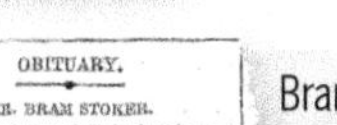

Bram dies April 20, five days after the sinking of the Titanic

1912

Literary auction at Sothebys, 317 items of Bram's personal library

1913

Dracula's Guest and Other Weird Stories, Routledge, London, Florence Stoker

1914

1922

First Dramatic production of *Dracula* by Hamilton Deane at the Grand Theatre in Derby

1924

1925

Florence Stoker and The Society of Authors win judgement (1922-25) against Prana Films on copyright infringement of *Nosferatu*

Tod Browning directed movie *Dracula* with Bela Lugosi

1927

1962

Biography of Dracula: Bram Stoker by Harry Ludlam

The Man Who Wrote Dracula: A Biography of Bram Stoker by Daniel Farson

1975

Bram Stoker: A Biography of the Author of Dracula by Barbara Belford

1996

Beyond Dracula by William Hughes

2000

2004

From the Shadow of Dracula by Paul Murray

Something in the Blood by David Skal

2016

NOTES AND NUGGETS

During my years of research into the background and history of *Dracula*, and also into the history of Bram Stoker, I have come across many fascinating pieces of information. Here are a few of my favourites, which I hope readers might find similarly enticing.

Did You Know?

Bram included a lot of 'new' technology in *Dracula*. I believe he was making a statement: in order to defeat the 'old ways', one must understand and respect history and superstition but people must be able to harness the power of advancement.

Here's a few of the technological elements included in the book:

- Dr Seward's recording phonograph and wax cylinders.
- A searchlight in Whitby to assist the coastguard in rescues of crewmen on shipwrecks.
- The typewriter that Mina used to write her notes and journals was very new at the time.
- Phrenology was an emerging science about the study of facial features linked to personality.
- Kodak camera photos that Harker took to show Count Dracula the properties which had been purchased on his behalf.

Mt Izvorul: The Location of Castle Dracula

The location of Bram's fictional castle in *Dracula* has been verified by close examination of Bram's notes for *Dracula* by researcher Hans de Roos. He recognised that Bram had actually written, on the corner of a piece of paper, the lines of longitude and latitude along with the names of nearby rivers and towns pin-pointing the top of Mt Izvorul in the Calimani National Park, as the location of Bram's fictional castle. The original ending of *Dracula*, prior to editing, involved a volcanic eruption following the demise of the Count. It's not surprising, therefore, to find out that Bram did his homework: it would only be fitting for a volcanic eruption to occur on a mountain that was at one time an active volcano, as was Mt Izvorul.

William Gladstone

William Gladstone was a British statesman and Liberal politician. In a career lasting over 60 years, he served for 12 years as Prime Minister of the United Kingdom, spread over four terms beginning in 1868 and ending in 1894. Bram obviously admired the man, and sent him a copy of *Dracula* on the twenty-fourth of May, 1897. Here is Bram's letter which accompanied that copy.

24 May 1897
My Dear Mr Gladstone,

May I do myself the pleasure of sending you a copy of my new novel *Dracula* which comes out on the 26th. Perhaps at your leisure you may honour me by reading it.

It is a story of a vampire – the old medieval vampire but recrudescent today. It has I think pretty well all the vampire legends as to limitations and these may interest you who have made in some way a bold guess at 'immortaliability'.

The book is necessarily full of horrors and terrors but I trust that these are calculated to cleanse the mind by pity & terror. At any rate there is nothing base in the book, and though superstition is brought in with the weapons of superstition, I hope it is not irrelevant. You will I know pardon my adding to the labour of your life by even the reading of one more letter. My regard for you and your work through all my thinking life has been such that I deem it a high privilege to be able to address you in the first person and to be able to put before you a book of my own, though it be only an atom in the intellectual kingdom where you have as long held sway.

Believe me
Your very sincere and respectful friend
Bram Stoker

Celebrity Quotes in *Dracula*

Like any good writer, Bram Stoker effectively used elements of the 'real world' in his fiction which included everything from locations and technology to quotes and references to friends and family and those he admired.

Here are two choice examples:

From Bram's good friend and neighbour in Chelsea, Mark Twain:

'I heard once of an American who so defined faith, that faculty which enables us to believe things which we know to be untrue.'

This appears in Chapter 14 and is paraphrasing from Twain's 1897 book *Following the Equator*: 'There are those who scoff at the schoolboy, calling him frivolous and shallow: yet it was the schoolboy who said faith is believing what you know ain't so.'

And, from an article in the *New York World Newspaper* 1896, a copy of which was found in Bram Stoker's papers. This piece referenced naturalist Charles Darwin, author of *Origin of the Species* (1859).

'Belief in the vampire bat is more modern. For a long time it was ridiculed by science as a delusion, but it has been proved to be found correctly in fact. It was the famous naturalist Darwin who settled this question. One night he was camping with a party near Coquimbo Chili and it happened that a servant noticed the restlessness of one of the horses. The man went up to the horse and actually caught a bat in the act of sucking blood from the flank of the animal. While many kinds of bats have been ignorantly accused of the bloodsucking habit only one species is really a vampire. It constitutes a genus all by itself.'

Bram uses the essence of Darwin's discovery of the vampire bat when Quincey Morris uses very similar words to describe the blood sucking bats in *Dracula*. Here's the section from Chapter 12 where Quincey recounts his days in South America:

'I have not seen anything pulled down so quick since I was on the Pampas and had a mare that I was fond of go to grass all in a night. One of those big bats that they call vampires had got at her during the night and what with his gorge and the vein left open, there wasn't enough blood in her to let her stand up.'

Later in Chapter 14 Bram has Van Helsing utter similar words when trying to convince Dr Seward of the presence of vampire bats:

'Can you tell me why in the Pampas, ay and elsewhere, there are bats that come out at night and open the veins of cattle and horses and suck dry their veins, how in some islands of the Western seas there are bats which hang on the trees all day, and those who have seen describe as like giant nuts or pods, and that when the sailors sleep on the deck, because that it is hot, flit down on them and then in the morning are found dead men, white as even Miss Lucy was?'

'Good God, Professor!' I said, starting up. 'Do you mean to tell me that Lucy was bitten by such a bat, and that such a thing is here in London in the nineteenth century?'

The London Library Discovery, 2018

We know Bram did not travel to Transylvania when he researched locations for Count Dracula's lair, and our knowledge of his research source was always quite limited. But that changed in 2018, when Philip Spedding discovered a trove of Bram's research material in The London Library and caused a lot of excitement in the world of 'Dracula studies'. As the Library's website explains:

'The London Library today unveiled a fascinating discovery that sheds new light on how *Dracula* was researched and written. We've found 26 books that are almost certainly the original copies that Bram Stoker used to help research his enduring classic.

'Philip Spedding, the Library's Development Director who made the discovery, commented: "Bram Stoker was a member of The London Library but until now we have had no indication whether or how he used our collection. Today's discovery changes that and we can establish beyond reasonable doubt that numerous books still on our shelves are the very copies that he was using to help write and research his masterpiece.

'Philip's detective trail began with the collection of Stoker's handwritten and typed notes that had been discovered in 1913 but only published in facsimile form in 2008. The notes list a wide range of Stoker's sources for *Dracula* and include hundreds of references to individual lines and phrases that he considered relevant. A recent trawl of our shelves has revealed that the Library has original copies of 25 of these books, carrying detailed markings that closely match Stoker's notebook references.'

I was able to assist Philip in verifying that the 'detailed markings' were made by Bram's hand – and it was interesting to see that among the books Bram marked most heavily were Sabine Baring-Gould's *The Book of Were-Wolves* and Thomas *Browne's Pseudodoxica Epidemica*.

Philip's discovery answered the many questions about what Bram *may* have read during his research process for *Dracula*, and confirmed that Stoker went into great detail with his historical and research in sources like: A F Crosse's *Round About the Carpathians* and *Charles Boner's Transylvania: Its Products and Its People*.

The Library has also established that their collection contains books with comparable handwritten notes that were not listed as sources in Bram's notes; and that some of the books mentioned in Bram's notes are no longer on the Library's shelves.

This list of titles are the books actually used by Bram and still in The London Library, and includes travel guides, maps, and information about Vampirism, Mesmerism, and Superstitions:

* *Nineteenth Century XVIII*, Mme Emily de Laszowka Gerard, Kegan Paul, Trench & Co, July 1885
* *The Book of Were-Wolves*, Sabine Baring-Gould, Smith, Elder and Co, 1865
* *Pseudodoxia Epidemica*, Thomas Browne, 1672
* *Magyarland*, Nina Elizabeth Mazuchelli, Sampson Low, Marston, Searle & Rivington, 1881
* *The Golden Chersonese*, Isabella Bird, John Murray, 1883
* *Round about the Carpathians*, A F Crosse, Blackwoods, 1878
* *On the Track of Crescent*, Major E C Johnson, Hurst & Blackett, 1885
* *Transylvania: Its Products and Its People*, Charles Boner, Longman,

Green, Reader & Dyer, 1865
- *An Account of the Principalities of Wallachia and Moldavia*, William Wilkinson, Longman, Hurst, Rees, Orme & Brown, 1820
- *Curious Myths of the Middle Ages* (2 vol), Sabine Baring-Gould, Rivington, 1868
- *Germany Past and Present* (2 vol), Sabine Baring-Gould, C Kegan Paul & Co, 1879
- *Legends and Superstitions of the Sea and of Sailors*, Fletcher S Bassett, Belford, Clarke & Co, 1885
- *The Origin of Primitive Superstitions*, Dorman, Lippincott, 1881
- *Credulities Past & Present*, W Jones, Chatto & Windus, 1880
- *The Folk-Tales of The Magyars*, The Rev W Henry Jones and Lewis L Kropf, The Folk-Lore Society, 1889
- *Superstition & Force*, H C Lea, Lea Brothers & Co, 1892
- *Sea Fables Explained*, Henry Lee, William Cloves & Sons, 1883
- *Anecdotes of the Habits and Instincts of Birds, Reptiles and Fishes*, Mrs R Lee, Grant & Griffith, 1853
- *The Other World; or, Glimpses of the Supernatural Being Facts, Records, and Traditions*, F G Lee, Henry S King & Co, 1875
- *Letters on the Truths Contained in Popular Superstitions*, Herbert Mayo, Blackwood, 1849
- *The Devil: His Origin, Greatness and Decadence*, Rev Albert Réville, Williams & Norgate, 1871
- *A Tarantasse Journey through Eastern Russia in the Autumn of 1856*, W Spottiswode, Longman, Brown, Green, Longmans & Roberts, 1857
- *The Spottiswoode Miscellany*, W Spottiswode, 1844
- *Traité des Superstitions qui Regardent les Sacraments* (4 vol), Jean-Baptiste Thiers, Louis Chambeau, 1777
- *The Phantom World: or, The Philosophy of Spirits, Apparitions &c.* (2 vol), Augustin Calmet, Richard Bentley, 1850
- *The Land Beyond the Forest* (2 vol), E Gerard, William Blackwood & Sons, 1888

Cruden Bay, Aberdeenshire, Scotland

Mike Shepherd, retired geologist and present day author with a deep-rooted interest in the history of his birthplace Aberdeenshire, has in the last several years turned his interest towards Bram Stoker and his connection with the area. According to Mike, Stoker stumbled upon Port Errol completely by chance. He had heard that the Aberdeenshire air was 'very bracing' and noted in his diaries that when he first saw the place, he fell in love with it. It was well-known that Bram visited 'a few times', staying at the Kilmarnock Arms with Florence and Noel and sometimes in cottages he rented. Significantly, Mike's diligence verified that Bram spent at least thirteen of his month-long summer holidays in and around Cruden Bay, known in Bram's day as the village of Port Errol. Most of the summers between 1893-1910 were spent writing two books based on local lore: *The Mystery of the Sea* and *The Watters Mou'*. Mike realised that Bram not only wrote large portions of *Dracula* here, it was also in Cruden Bay that he edited the 1897 edition of *Dracula* to condense the text and create the 1901 abridged edition of *Dracula*.

I have had the pleasure of visiting Mike on three different occasions in the charming town of Cruden Bay. Each time I am struck

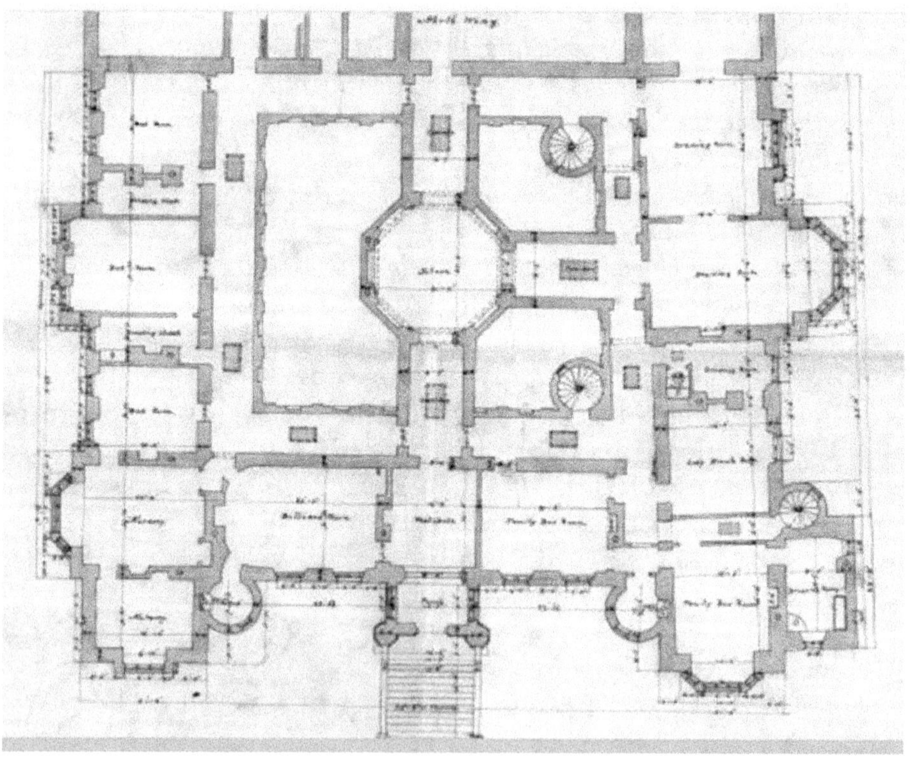

Floor Plan of Slains Castle

by the realisation that this fairly remote area of northern Scotland has changed very little since my great grand-uncle spent his summer holidays there. Mike identified for me the obvious landmarks and local residents who had aspects of their lives recreated in Bram's fiction, and took great pleasure in sharing with me what he had learned by comparing Bram's descriptions of fictional landscapes with the actual coastline. Mike recognised specific rock formations and seascapes Bram described and the vantage points from which Bram wrote his notes and with Mike I had the great fortune to walk

The octagonal room in Slains Castle as it exists today.

along the same beach and explore the rocky cliffs and caves that Bram described.

Mike fully explains Bram Stoker's Scottish connections in his book *When Brave Men Shudder* (2018). The book neatly links Stoker's Cruden Bay experiences to specific passages in his writing – the most famous of which has to be the famed octagonal room in Slains Castle, described by Bram in Chapter 2 of *Dracula* as the octagonal room through which Count Dracula led Jonathan Harker *en route* to his bedroom in the castle.

Bram Stoker Writes with the Eye Of A Painter

Bram was a founding member of the Dublin Painting and Sketching Club which was founded in 1874 by a small group of professional and amateur artists. The group aimed to bring artists together, hold public exhibitions and stimulate artistic taste. The founding group included Dr William Stokes FRS, President of the Royal Academy and Bram Stoker. Alfred Grey became the first President and Alexander Williams the first Hon Secretary, both were academicians of the Royal Hibernian Academy (RHA).

Many of Ireland's leading artists of the time became members, including John Butler Yeats, Walter Osborne and Nathaniel Hone.

Later Sarah Purser, Richard Moynan and Bingham McGuinness joined: all were academicians of the RHA.

The fact that Bram was an amateur artist does explain to a certain extent his 'eye' for landscapes and his ability to describe landscapes in such accurate detail. I also believe that his artistic nature contributed to descriptions of his fictional Castle Dracula, which incorporated two sketches of Bran Castle Bram saw in books by E Mazuchelli and C Boner.

Letter from Arthur Conan Doyle to Bram Stoker

Aug 20/97

My dear Bram Stoker

I am sure that you will not think it an impertinence if I write to tell you how very much I have enjoyed reading *Dracula*. I think it is the very best story of diablerie which I have read for many years. It is really wonderful how with so much exciting interest over so long a book there is never an anticlimax. It holds you from the very start and grows more and more engrossing until it is quite painfully vivid. The old Professor is most excellent and so are the two girls. I congratulate you with all my heart for having written so fine a book.

With all kindest remembrances to Mrs Bram Stoker and yourself.

Yours very truly
A Conan Doyle

What Winston Churchill Said About Bram Stoker

The following exchange is noted in regard to a 1908 interview with Winston Churchill conducted by Bram Stoker and published in the *Daily Chronicle*, London, on 15 January. This was only the second interview ever permitted by Churchill, who was at the time a member of the Liberal Party and notoriously journalist-shy. The interview was granted as Bram had known Churchill's father. The website winstonchurchill.org explains: 'It was around 1887, according to Stoker, when Lord Randolph introduced him to thirteen-year-old Winston: "He's not much yet, you know. But he's a good 'un. He's a good 'un!" And, Stoker adds, "a 'good 'un' he turned out to be."'

'When I wrote to Mr Winston Churchill asking for an appointment to interview him he replied: "I would very much rather not; but if you wish it I cannot refuse you."

'When I met him in his library he explained more fully: "I hate being interviewed, and I have refused altogether to allow it. But I have to break the rule for you, for you were a friend of my father." Then he added gracefully another reason personal to myself: "And because you are the author of *Dracula*."'

The Original Ending of *Dracula*

When analysing the *Dracula* typescript I found that there was indeed almost a full page of text crossed out at the end of the novel. This was most interesting to me because of the material which was deleted.

The ending as we know it involves a fierce battle between the 'band of heroes' and the gypsies who are guarding Count Dracula as he is transported back to his castle in his crate carried by a leiter wagon. The heroes confront the gypsies, manage to fight them off, and are able to open the crate holding the Count. Jonathan Harker cuts the throat of the Count with a Kukri blade while Quincey Morris stabs the Count in the heart with his Bowie knife. At this point the Count gets a look of peace on his face, crumbles into dust and disappears.

Mina Harker remarks in her journal that within minutes a massive volcanic eruption occurs and causes the nearby Castle Dracula to tumble into pieces.

Did Bram change the ending or did his editor? Did Bram purposely give Quincey Morris a Bowie knife to stab the Count instead of a wooden stake? Was this ending changed simply as a way to have a less than definitive ending for Count Dracula and allow Bram to set up a future sequel?

The original ending of *Dracula* can be found in the Telos edition of the novel amongst other places online.

INTERVIEW WITH BRAM STOKER

Despite the fact that he was an author and penned a number of books following the release of *Dracula*, it would appear that Bram Stoker was rarely asked about his vampire novel. In fact, at this point only one interview is known to exist in which he talks about the book.

Dracula was published on May 26, 1897. This interview, conducted by Jane T Stoddart ('Lorna'), was published in the *British Weekly*, 1 July 1897, p. 185.

Mr Bram Stoker. A Chat With The Author Of *Dracula*

One of the most interesting and exciting of recent novels is Mr Bram Stoker's *Dracula*. It deals with the ancient mediaeval vampire legend, and in no English work of fiction has this legend been so brilliantly treated. The scene is laid partly in Transylvania and partly in England. The first fifty-four pages, which give the journal of Jonathan Harker after leaving Vienna until he makes up his mind to escape from Castle Dracula, are in their weird power altogether unrivalled in recent fiction. The only book which to my knowledge at all compares with them is *The Waters of Hercules*, by E D Gerard, which also treats of a wild and little known portion of Eastern Europe. Without revealing the plot of the story, I may say that Jonathan Harker, whose diary first introduces the vampire Count, is a young solicitor sent by his employer to Castle Dracula to arrange for the purchase of a house and estate in England.

From the first day of his starting, signs and wonders follow him.

At the Golden Krone at Bistritz the landlady warns him not to go to Castle Dracula, and, finding that his purpose is unalterable, places a rosary with a crucifix round his neck. For this gift he has good cause to be grateful afterwards. Harker's fellow-passengers on the stage-coach grow more and more alarmed about his safety as they come nearer to the dominions of the Count. Kindly gifts are pressed upon him: wild rose, garlic, and mountain ash. These are meant to be a protection against the evil eye. The author seems to know every corner of Transylvania and all its superstitions. Presently in the Borgo Pass a carriage with four horses drives up beside the coach. 'The horses were driven by a tall man with a long brown beard, and a great black hat which seemed to hide his face from us. I could only see the gleam of a pair of very bright eyes, which seemed red in the lamplight as he turned to us … As he spoke he smiled, and the lamplight fell on a hard-looking mouth, with very red lips and sharp-looking teeth as white as ivory. One of my companions whispered the line from Burger's *Lenore*: "Denn die Todten reiten schnell" ("For the dead travel fast").'

This is the famous king vampire, Count Dracula, in ancient times a warlike Transylvanian noble. Jonathan Harker is conscious from the first that he is among ghostly and terrible surroundings. Even on the night journey to the Castle, wolves which have gathered round the carriage disappear when the terrible driver lifts his hand. On his arrival the guest is left waiting, and presently a tall old man, whom he suspects from the beginning to be none other than the driver himself, bids him welcome to his house. The Count never eats with his guest. During the day he is absent, but during the night he converses, the dawn breaking up the interview. There are no mirrors to be seen in any part of the ancient building, and the young solicitor's fears are confirmed by the fact that one morning, when the Count comes unexpectedly to his bedroom and stands looking over his shoulder, there is no reflection of him in the small shaving glass Harker has brought from London, and which covers the whole room behind.

The adventures of Jonathan Harker will be read again and again; the most powerful part of the book after this is the description of the voyage of the *Demeter* from Varna to Whitby. A supernatural terror haunts the crew from the moment that they leave the Dardanelles, and as time goes on one man after another disappears. It is whispered that at night a man, tall, thin, and ghastly pale, is seen moving about the ship. The mate, a Roumanian, who probably knows the vampire legend, searches during the day in a number of old boxes, and in one he finds Count Dracula asleep. His own suicide and the death of the captain follow, and when the ship arrives at Whitby, the vampire escapes in the form of a huge dog. The strange thing is that, although in some respects this is a gruesome book, it leaves on the mind an entirely wholesome impression. The events which happen are so far removed from ordinary experience that they do not haunt the imagination unpleasantly. It is certain that no other writer of our day could have produced so marvellous a book.

On Monday morning I had the pleasure of a short conversation with Mr Bram Stoker, who, as most people know, is Sir Henry Irving's manager at the Lyceum Theatre. He told me, in reply to a question, that the plot of the story had been a long time in his mind, and that he spent about three years in writing it. He had always been interested in the vampire legend. 'It is undoubtedly,' he remarked, 'a very fascinating theme, since it touches both on mystery and fact. In the Middle Ages the terror of the vampire depopulated whole villages.'

'Is there any historical basis for the legend?'
'It rested, I imagine, on some such case as this. A person may have fallen into a death-like trance and been buried before the time. Afterwards the body may have been dug up and found alive, and from this a horror seized upon the people, and in their ignorance they imagined that a vampire was about. The more hysterical, through excess of fear, might themselves fall into trances in the same way; and so the story grew that one vampire might enslave many others and make them like himself. Even in the single villages it was believed that there might be many such creatures. When once the panic seized the population, their only thought was to escape.'

'In what parts of Europe has this belief been most prevalent?'
'In certain parts of Styria it has survived longest and with most intensity, but the legend is common to many countries, to China, Iceland, Germany, Saxony, Turkey, the Chersonese, Russia, Poland, Italy, France, and England, besides all the Tartar communities.'

'In order to understand the legend, I suppose it would be necessary to consult many authorities?'
Mr Stoker told me that the knowledge of vampire superstitions shown in *Dracula* was gathered from a great deal of miscellaneous reading.

'No one book that I know of will give you all the facts. I learned a good deal from E Gerard's *Essays on Roumanian Superstitions*, [sic] which first appeared in the Nineteenth Century, and were afterwards published in a couple of volumes. I also learned something from Mr Baring-Gould's *Were-Wolves*. Mr Gould has promised a book on vampires, but I do not know whether he has made any progress with it.'

Readers of *Dracula* will remember that the most famous character in it is Dr Van Helsing, the Dutch physician, who, by extraordinary skill, self-devotion, and labour, finally outwits and destroys the vampire. Mr Stoker told me that van Helsing is founded on a real character. In a recent leader on *Dracula*, published in a provincial newspaper, it is suggested that high moral lessons might be gathered from the book. I asked Mr Stoker whether he had written with a purpose, but on this point he would give no definite answer, 'I suppose that every book of the kind must contain some lesson,' he remarked; 'but I prefer that readers should find it out for themselves.'

In reply to further questions, Mr Stoker said that he was born in Dublin, and that his work had laid for thirteen years in the Civil Service. He is an MA of Trinity College, Dublin. His brother-in-law is Mr Frankfort Moore, one of the most popular young writers of the day. He began his literary work early. The first thing he published was a book on *The Duties of Clerks of Petty Sessions*. Next came a series of children's stories, *Under the Sunset*, published by Sampson Low. Then followed the book by which he has hitherto been best known, *The Snake's Pass*. Messrs Constable have published in their *Acme* library a fascinating little volume called *The Watter's Mou'*, and this with *The Shoulder of Shasta*, completes Mr Stoker's list of novels. He has been in London for some nineteen years, and believes that London is the best possible place for a literary man. 'A writer will find a chance here if he is good for anything; and recognition is only a matter of time.' Mr Stoker speaks of the generosity shown by literary men to one another in a tone which shows that he, at least, is not disposed to quarrel with the critics.

Mr Stoker does not find it necessary to publish through a literary agent. It always seems to him, he says, that an author with an ordinary business capacity can do better for himself than through any agent. 'Some men now-a-days are making ten thousand a year by their novels, and it seems hardly fair that they should pay ten or five percent of this great sum to a middleman. By a dozen letters or so in the course of the year they could settle all their literary business on their own account.' Though Mr Stoker did not say so, I am inclined to think that the literary agent is to him a nineteenth century vampire.

No interview during this week would be complete without a reference to the Jubilee, so I asked Mr Stoker, as a Londoner of nearly twenty years standing, what he thought of the celebrations. 'Everyone,' he said, 'has been proud that the great day went off so successfully. We have had a magnificent survey of the Empire, and last week's procession brought home, as nothing else could have done, the sense of the immense variety of the Queen's dominions.'

EXCERPTS FROM OBITUARIES OF BRAM STOKER

I find it very interesting to read what his peers wrote about Bram Stoker in his obituaries which are not just tributes, but also important records of biographical information for researchers like myself. Like an interesting eulogy given at a funeral, I appreciate the personal remembrances and anecdotes shared in some obituaries. Through these selections, much can be learned about how Bram was regarded

Excerpt from Bram Stoker's *New York Times* Obituary, 23 April 1912

He was a tall blond Irishman who had been well educated in Dublin, and had filled small positions in the civil service. But he had theatrical inclinations, and had once applied to Mr and Mrs Kendal for employment as business manager. They felt afterward that they had reason to regret their refusal to employ him.

Yet he might never have had the success in that field with another employer than Irving. The great actor and his associate had long been friends. Irving placed implicit confidence in Stoker's judgement and business sense, while Stoker looked upon Irving as the only supremely great man in the world. Their relationship lasted from the beginning of Irving's career as manager of the London Lyceum until his death.

Stoker relieved Irving of every possible care, was the active host at the famous supper parties, stood between Irving and the crowd of theater aspirants and would-be playwrights. He paid the bills and arranged all the details of the transportation.

He was never tired and never depressed. He remembered the faces and names of all he ever met, or, if he did not, he had the skill to make others believe he did. Undoubtedly much of Irving's success was due to him.

For the rest he wrote fluently and was eagerly interested in all the affairs of the world. Deep down in his nature there was a touch of Celtic mysticism. It sought expression in literary form, but his stories though they were queer were not of a memorable quality. His *Life of Irving* however, is a noteworthy book.

He had plenty of friends and enough enemies to indicate that his friendship was worth having. The embodiment of health and strength and geniality, it seems he died too young. He was only 64 years of age. Almost everyone who knew him will say that he should have lived to be 90 and kept a young heart in his old age.

'Death of Mr Bram Stoker', *The Irish Times*, 22 April 1912

The Times announces the death on Saturday evening at his London residence, after a long illness, of Mr Bram Stoker, who for nearly thirty years was Sir Henry Irving's manager and confidential secretary. He wrote, it will be remembered, the great actor's biography.

The late Mr Stoker was the son of the late Mr Abraham Stoker, of Chief Secretary's Office, Dublin Castle, and brother of Sir Thornley Stoker, and was educated at Trinity College, Dublin. He entered the Irish Civil Service Registrar of Petty Sessions Clerks' Department of the Chief Secretary's Office, Dublin Castle, where he remained until 1878, being Inspector of Petty Sessions in Ireland during the years 1877-1878. He had a distinguished career in Dublin University, and was literary, art, and dramatic critic on the staff of various journals. He was a Barrister of an Inner Temple, and the author of many books.

Pall Mall Gazette (London), 22 April 1912
Sir Henry Irving's Secretary

The Times this morning announces the death of Mr Bram Stoker, who for nearly thirty years was the intimate friend of Sir Henry Irving. Mr Stoker had been ill since 1906, and he passed away on Saturday evening at 26, St George's Square.

Bram, or baptismally, Abraham, Stoker was born in Dublin in 1847, his father Abraham being one of the officials in the Chief

Secretary's Department in the Castle. He was educated at Trinity College, where he won honours in science, mathematics, oratory, history, and composition, besides distinguishing himself as a sportsman and debater. He was for some time in the Irish Civil Service as inspector of Petty Sessions, and was engaged in journalism as well, both as editor of an evening paper and as a dramatic critic. In 1876 or thereabouts he first came into contact with Henry Irving, and two years later he had permanently thrown in his lot with him as his manager and confidential secretary, and he remained with him until the end.

The *Daily Telegraph*, 24 April 1912
By Thomas Hall Caine
Bram Stoker: The Story of a Great Friendship

Bram Stoker is to be buried today. The remains will be cremated at Golder's Green Crematorium. Only the friends (and they are many) who know and loved him will be there when the last offices are done, and that will be enough. He could have desired no more and no better. The big, breathless, impetuous hurricane of a man who was Bram Stoker had no love of the limelight …

… When I think of his literary output I regret the loss of the one book with which he might have enriched the literature of autobiography. The multitude of interesting persons with whom his position brought him into contact – Tennyson, Disraeli, Gladstone, Randolph Churchill, Archbishop Benson, President Cleveland, Walt Whitman, Rénan – had left him with a vast store of memories which the public would have welcomed if he had written them down. He never did write them, and the world is the poorer for want of his glimpses, however brief and casual, of some of its great souls in their happiest hours.

In concluding this little and imperfect tribute to the memory of a massive and muscular and almost volcanic personality that must have been familiar by sight to many thousands in Great Britain and America, I could wish to end where I began with the warmest and most affectionate recognition of his genius for friendship. No one knows better than the friend to whom, under various disguises (impenetrable to all except themselves), he dedicated in words of love some of his best-known books (*Dracula* in particular), how large was the heart that was not entirely exhausted even by the devotion to the great man with whom his name is generally associated. There were moments during the past twenty-odd years when I felt ashamed that anybody should give me his time, his energy, and his enthusiasm as Bram gave them, and the only way in which I could reconcile myself to his splendid self-sacrifice was to remember that he loved to make it. I can think of nothing – absolutely nothing – that I could have asked Bram Stoker to do for me that he would not have done. It is only once in a man's life that such a friendship comes to him, and when the grave is closed on the big heart which we are to bury to-day, I shall feel that I have lost it.

Of the devotion of his wife during these last dark days, in which the whirlwind of his spirit had nothing lost to it but the broken wreck of a strong man, I cannot trust myself to speak. That must always be a sacred memory to those who knew what it was. If his was the genius of friendship, hers must have been the genius of love.

REVIEWS OF *DRACULA:* SELECTED EXCERPTS

When looking back on contemporary reviews, it becomes apparent that *Dracula* was not immediately recognised as the classic novel it would become. Overall the response was positive, but there some who found the more *gothic* elements too much to bear. In fact very much like the novel is regarded today.

I think it is fair to say that over one hundred years ago, no one could imagine that *Dracula*, would still be in print, much less still inspiring countless films, literary adaptations, study and research papers and commercial products.

Additional reviews of *Dracula* can be found in John Edgar Browning's book *Bram Stoker's Dracula: The Critical Feast (2011)* The Apocryphile Press

Detroit Free Press, **18 November 1899**
'Bram Stoker's Story'

It is almost inconceivable that Bram Stoker wrote *Dracula*. Still, he must have done it. There is his name on the title page, and before the tale was bound up and offered us between covers it ran its length in various newspapers, and under the same name of authorship.

So there is no getting around it. Bram Stoker did write it.

Think of the story. It is a tale of ghouls, vampires and human imps all in direct communication with Satan. There are lunatics and idiots in it who feed flies to spiders, spiders to sparrows, and then, in lieu of a cat, devour the sparrows themselves. A weird count – the Dracula from whom the book is named – lives in a castle high among the Carpathians and weaves webs for ordinary folk – casts spells over pretty girls, and draws the strings tighter until they die – the girls, that is. An amazing man – Dracula. To achieve his fiendish ends he assumes many and divers forms. Now he is a spirit, visible but untangible, with two sharp front teeth and red eyes. Again he is a dog, then a bat, in turn a wolf at last. As a bat, he goes about biting people in the neck. Of course they die. A Dutch specialist in physiological psychology sets out to solve the mystery of the strange deaths. In the end Dracula is worsted. His head is cut off and a stake is driven through his heart. There's an outline of the tale – such is what you may hope to find between the covers.

And it is a splendid story, too; done in a manner most convincing – by letters, diaries. And medical observations.

And Bram Stoker wrote it!

Think of him.

He – a great, shambling, good-natured, overgrown boy – although he is the business manager of Henry Irving and the Lyceum Theatre – with a red beard, untrimmed, and a ruddy complexion, tempered somewhat by the wide-open full blue eyes that gaze so frankly into yours! Why, it is hard enough to imagine Bram Stoker a business man, to say nothing of his possessing an imagination capable of projecting *Dracula* upon paper.

But he has done it. And he has done it well.

If you enjoy the weird, if you care for spinal titillations, *Dracula* is unstintingly recommended.

The Manchester Guardian, 15 June 1897

A writer who attempts in the nineteenth century to rehabilitate the ancient legends of the were-wolf and the vampire has set himself a formidable task. Most of the delightful old superstitions of the past have an unhappy way of appearing limp and sickly in the glare of a later day, and in such a story as *Dracula*, by Bram Stoker, the reader must reluctantly acknowledge that the region of horrors has shifted its ground. Man is no longer in dread of the monstrous and the unnatural, and although Mr Stoker has tackled his gruesome subject with enthusiasm, the effect is more often grotesque than terrible. The Transylvanian site of Castle Dracula is skilfully chosen, and the picturesque region is well described. Count Dracula himself has been in his day a medieval noble, who, by reason of his 'Vampire' qualities, is unable to die properly, but from century to century resuscitates his life of the 'Un-Dead', as the author terms it, by nightly draughts of blood from the throats of living victims, with the appalling consequence that those once so bitten must become vampire in their turn. The plot is too complicated for reproduction, but it says no little for the author's powers that in spite of its absurdities the reader can follow the story with interest to the end. It is, however, an artistic mistake to fill a whole volume with horrors. A touch of the mysterious, the terrible, or the supernatural is infinitely more effective and credible.

The Wave (San Francisco) 9 December 1899
'The Insanity of the Horrible'

When an Englishman, or, for that matter, anyone of Anglo-Saxon blood, goes into degenerate literature of his own sort, he reveals a horrible kind of degeneracy. The works of the French degenerates possess a *verve*, a Gaelic attractiveness, indefinable but yet definite, the same subtle quality which, in another line, makes every Frenchwoman, young or old, attractive with a charm that pertains to the soul and not to the body or the mind. Now it goes without saying that the Anglo-Saxon has no such quality. When he becomes degenerate, it is degeneracy of a terrible sort – coarse, brutal, unlovely, its only attraction the fascination of horror. The difference is that between Whitechapel and the Moulin Rouge. I make no doubt that the existence of a Moulin Rouge in its midst is a greater menace to a people than the existence of a Whitechapel, but between the relative attractiveness of the two there is and can be no comparison at all. Swift and Hogarth are two very horrible examples of the Anglo-Saxon method of treating those things which our modern conventionalities decree shall be hidden.

Dracula, by an Englishman who calls himself 'Bram Stoker', is an awful example. Here is a man who has taken the most horrible theme he could find in ancient or modern literature, the tradition regarding ghouls, or vampires, the beings, neither living nor dead, who creep in by night to suck the blood and damn the souls of their victims. He has then gone on to carry the thing out to all possible lengths. The plain horror were enough, perhaps, but the author goes farther, and adds insane asylums, dissecting rooms and unnatural appetites galore. No detail is too nauseating. In the first seventy pages, there are four cases of deaths caused by the preying of human vampires, one murder, one suicide, one lunatic with homicidal mania and a habit of eating flies, one somnambulist, one shipwreck, extent of fatalities not fully reported, one death by hysterical fright. Pleasant, isn't it? Well, these are only a sort of foretaste of incidents which I, being of a tender conscience, will forbear to harness on the imaginations of others.

There are two reasons of extended mention of this literary failure. The first is that the main cause of the failure shows so prominently as to furnish a beautiful object-lesson. This fault is the lack of artistic restraint. Stevenson, the century's greatest artist in fiction, happens to have used in two instances a theme like this one – in *Dr Jekyll and Mr Hyde*, and in the powerful short story 'Oliala'. And anyone who wishes the lesson should put these two masterpieces, where the horror is suggested, hinted at, written around except for the one moment of the climax when it is brought home with an added force derived from the very fact that it has been hidden so long against this systematic piling-up of all the unwholesome and unpleasant things in the world. The other thing which makes the book worthy of notice is the fact that, in spite of it all, it holds to the end. It is true that the fascination is the same as that which would be possessed by a dissecting room, but it is there nevertheless.

If you have the bad taste, after this warning, to attempt the book, you will read on to the finish, as I did – and go to bed, as I did, feeling furtively of your throat.

The Spectator 31 July 1897

Mr Bram Stoker gives us the impression – we may be doing him an injustice – of having deliberately laid himself out in *Dracula* to eclipse all previous efforts in the domain of the horrible – to 'go one better' than Wilkie Collins (whose method of narration he has closely followed), Sheridan Le Fanu, and all the other professors of the flesh-creeping school. Count Dracula, who gives his name to the book, is a Transylvanian noble who purchases an estate in England, and in connection with the transfer of the property Jonathan Harker, a young solicitor, visits him in his ancestral castle. Jonathan Harker has a terrible time of it, for the Count – who is a vampire of immense age, cunning and experience – keeps him as a prisoner forseveral weeks, and when the poor young man escapes from the gruesome charnel-house of his host, he nearly dies of brain-fever in a hospital at Budapest.

The scene then shifts to England, where the Count arrives by sea in the shape of a dog-fiend, after destroying the entire crew, and resumes operations in various uncanny manifestations, selecting as his chief victim Miss Lucy Westenra, the fiancée of the Honourable Arthur Holmwood, heir presumptive to Lord Godalming. The story then resolves itself into the history of the battle between Lucy's protectors, including two rejected suitors – an American and a 'mad' doctor – and a wonderfully clever specialist from Amsterdam, against her unearthly persecutor. The clue is furnished by Jonathan Harker, whose betrothed, Mina Murray, is a bosom friend of Lucy's, and the fight is long and protracted.

Lucy succumbs, and, worse still, is temporarily converted into a vampire. How she is released from this unpleasant position and restored to a peaceful post-mortem existence, how Mina is next assailed by the Count, how he is driven from England, and finally exterminated by the efforts of the league – for all these and a great many more thrilling details, we must refer our readers to the pages of Mr Stoker's clever but cadaverous romance. Its strength lies in the invention of incident, for the sentimental element is decidedly mawkish. Mr Stoker has shown considerable ability in the use that he has made of all the available traditions of vampirology, but we think his story would have been all the more effective if he had chosen an earlier period. The up-to-dateness of the book – the phonograph diaries, typewriters and so on – hardly fits in with the mediaeval methods which ultimately secure the victory for Count Dracula's foes.

The Daily Mail, 1 June 1897

It is said of Mrs Radcliffe that when writing her now almost forgotten romances she shut herself up in absolute seclusion, and fed upon raw beef, in order to give her work the desired atmosphere of gloom, tragedy and terror. If one had no assurance to the contrary one might well supposed that a similar method and regimen had been adopted by Mr Bram Stoker while writing his new novel *Dracula*. In seeking for a parallel to this weird, powerful, and horrorful story our mind reverts to such tales as *The Mysteries of Udolpho, Frankenstein, Wuthering Heights, The Fall of the House of Usher*, and *Marjery of Quether*. But *Dracula* is even more appalling in its gloomy fascination than any one of these.

We started reading it early in the evening, and followed Jonathan Harker on his mission to the Carpathians with no definite conjecture as to what waited us in the castle of Dracula. When we came to the night journey over the mountain road and were chased by the wolves, which the driver, with apparently miraculous power, repelled by a mere gesture, we began to scent mystery, but we were not perturbed. The first thrill of horrible sensation came with the discovery that the driver and the Count Dracula were one and the same person, that the count was the only human inhabitant of the castle, and that the rats, the bats, the ghosts, and the howling wolves were his familiars.

By ten o'clock the story had so fastened itself upon our attention that we could not pause even to light our pipe. At midnight the narrative had fairly got upon our nerves; a creepy terror had seized upon us, and when at length, in the early hours of the morning, we went upstairs to bed it was with the anticipation of nightmare. We listened anxiously for the sound of bats' wings against the window; we even felt at our throat in dread least an actual vampire should have left there the two ghastly punctures which in Mr Stoker's book attested to the hellish operations of Dracula.

The recollections of this weird and ghostly tale will doubtless haunt us for some time to come. It would be unfair to the author to divulge the plot. We therefore restrict ourselves to the statement that the eerie chapters are written and strung together with very considerable art and cunning, and also with unmistakable literary power. Tribute must also be paid to the rich imagination of which Mr Bram Stoker here gives liberal evidence. Persons of small courage and weak nerves should confine their reading of these gruesome pages strictly to the hours between dawn and sunset.

***Pall Mall Gazette*, 1 June 1897**

Mr Bram Stoker should have labelled his book 'For Strong Men Only', or words to that effect. Left lying carelessly around, it might get into the hands of your maiden aunt who believes devoutly in the man under the bed, or of the new parlourmaid with unsuspected hysterical tendencies. *Dracula* to such would be manslaughter. It is for the man with a sound conscience and digestion, who can turn out the gas and go to bed without having to look over his shoulder more than half a dozen times as he goes upstairs, or more than mildly wishing that he had a crucifix and some garlic handy to keep the vampires from getting at him. That is to say, the story deals with the Vampire King, and it is horrid and creepy to the last degree. It is also excellent, and one of the best things in the supernatural line that we have been lucky enough to hit upon.

Glasgow Herald, 10 June 1897

It is an eerie and gruesome tale which Mr Stoker tells, but it is much the best book he has written. The reader is held with a spell similar to that of Wilkie Collins's *Moonstone*, and indeed in many ways the form of narrative by diaries and letters and extracts from newspapers neatly fitted into each other recalls Wilkie Collins's style … Mr Stoker keeps his devilry well in hand, if such an expression is allowable; as strange event follows strange event, the narrative might in less skilful hands become intolerably improbable; but *Dracula* to the end seems only too reasonably and sanely possible. Henceforth we shall wreathe ourselves in garlic when opportunity offers, and firmly decline all invitations to visit out-of-the-way clients in castles in the South-East of Europe. *Dracula* is a first rate book of adventure.

Bookman, August, 1897

Since Wilkie Collins left us we have had no tale of mystery so liberal in manner and so closely woven. But with the intricate plot, and the methods of the narrative, the resemblance to the stories of the author of *The Woman in White* ceases; for the audacity and horror of *Dracula* are Mr Stoker's own. A summary of the book would shock and disgust, but we must own that, though here and there in the course of the tale we hurried over things with repulsion, we read nearly the whole thing with rapt attention. It is something of a triumph for the writer that neither the improbability, nor the unnecessary number of hideous incidents recounted of the man-vampire, are long foremost on the reader's mind, but that the interest of the danger, of the complications, of the pursuit of the villain, of human skill and courage pitted against inhuman wrong and superhuman strength, rises always to the top. Keep *Dracula* out of the way of nervous children, certainly; but a grown reader, unless he be of unserviceably delicate stuff, will both shudder and enjoy from p 35, when Harker sees the Count 'emerge from the window and begin to crawl down the castle wall over that dreadful abyss, *face down*, with his cloak spreading out around him like great wings.'

And to finish, a more contemporary review.

The Guardian website, 4 February 2014
'Dracula by Bram Stoker – review' by Milo

Dracula isn't a book, not anymore. Dracula is a name, a broad stereotyping of a character which encompasses many different components and interpretations of our favourite Count. Having been a fan of the concept of vampires for some time, earlier this year I was intrigued to return to the beginning of the vampire genre when I first picked up this book …

The main characters are all very well portrayed, each with a separate personality, quirks and role to play in the story. The story itself is heartbreaking, full of the emotion of the characters as they deal with life, death and love, this is beautifully realised. *Dracula* touches on many themes, savagery, love, religion, technology and xenophobia to name just a few. It leaves you thinking upon it for a long time afterwards and is required reading for any fan of horror or vampires. *Dracula* is to vampire novels as *A Study in Scarlet* is to detective novels: one of the first, greatest and the story which introduced the character for those genres. Dracula is THE vampire and the novel is THE vampire novel.

EXPERIENCES OF THE CHOLERA IN IRELAND 1832

Charlotte M B Stoker

During the time of Bram's childhood illness his mother told him this story about when she was a girl in Sligo. Later in his life, when his parents and two sisters were living in France, Bram asked his mother to write the story he remembered and send it to him. Which she did, in great detail – a copy of which still exists. Bram used her story as a basis for the short story 'The Invisible Giant' in his collection of children's stories *Under the Sunset* (1881). Charlotte's experiences in Sligo are also on the short list of inspirations for *Dracula*.

In the days of my early youth the world was shaken with the dread of a new and terrible plague which was desolating all lands as it passed through them, and so regular was its march that men could tell where next it would appear and almost to the day when it might be expected. It was the cholera, which for the first time appeared in Western Europe. Its bitter strange kiss, and man's want of experience or knowledge of its nature, or how best to resist its attacks, added, if anything could, to its horrors.

In those days I lived with my parents and brothers in a provincial town in the west of Ireland called Sligo. It was long before the time of railroads and (I think) of steamboats, as news travelled slowly. Rumours of the great plague broke on us from time to time, as men talk of far-off things which can never come near themselves, but gradually the terror grew on us as we heard of it coming nearer and nearer. 'It is in France,' they said. 'It is in Germany,' and 'It is in England.'

Then, with wild affright, we began to hear the whisper passed, 'It is in Ireland!' Men's senses began failing them for fear, and deeds were done, in selfish dread, enough to call down God's direct vengeance on us.

One action I vividly remember. A poor traveller was taken ill on the roadside some miles from the town, and how did those samaritans tend him? They dug a pit and with long poles pushed him living into it, and covered him up quick, alive. Severely, like Sodom, did our city pay for such crimes.

Trenches were now cut across the roads in the direction in which the cholera was said to come, concisely for the purpose of stopping all intercourse with the infected districts. No use, no use!

One evening we heard that a Mrs Feeny, a very fat woman who was a music teacher, had died suddenly and, by the doctor's orders, had been buried an hour after. With blanched faces men looked at each other and whispered 'Cholera!'; but the whispers next day deepened to a roar, and in many houses lay one, nay two or three dead. One house would be attacked and the next spared. There was no telling who would go next, and when one said goodbye to a friend he said it as if for ever.

In a very few days the town became a place of the dead. No vehicles moved except the cholera carts or doctors' carriages. Many people fled, and many of these were overtaken by the plague and died by the way. Some of the doctors 'made a good thing of it' as they said themselves, at first, but one by one they too became victims, and others came and filled the gaps, and then others again filled their places.

Most of the clergy of all denominations fled, and few indeed were the instances in which the funeral service was read over the dead.

The great County Infirmary and Fever Hospital was turned into a cholera hospital, but was quite insufficient to meet the requirements of the situation. The nurses died one after another, and none could be found to fill their places but women of the worst description, who were always more than half drunk, and such scenes were perpetrated there as would make the flesh creep to hear of.

One Roman Catholic priest remained (there may have been others, I but knew of this one). His name was Gilern, and he told us himself that he was obliged to sit day after day, and night after night, on the top of the great stone stairs with a horse whip, to prevent those wretches dragging the patients down the stairs by the legs with their heads dashing on the stone steps, before they were dead.

The habit was when a new batch arrived for whom there were no beds, to take those who were stupified from opium and nearest death and remove them to make room for the new arrivals. Many were said to be buried alive. One man brought his wife to the hospital on his back and, she being in great agony, he tied a red scarf tightly round her waist to try and relieve the pain. When he came again to the hospital in the evening he heard that she was dead, and lying in the dead house. He sought her body to give it more decent burial than could be given there (the custom was to dig a large trench, put in forty or fifty corpses without coffins, throw lime on them and cover the grave). He saw the corner of his red scarf under several bodies which he removed, found his wife and saw there was still life in her. He carried her home and she recovered and lived many years.

There was a remarkable character in the town, a man of great stature, who had been a soldier and was usually known as 'long Sergeant Callen'. He took the cholera, was thought dead, and a coffin was brought. As the coffin maker had always a stack of coffins ready on hand, with the burials following immediately on the deaths, they were much of a uniform size and, of course, too short for long Sergeant Callen. The men who were putting him in, when they found he would not fit, took a big hammer to break his legs and make him fit. The first blow roused the sergeant from his stupor, and he started up and recovered. I often saw the man afterwards.

Our own household gradually ceased to go out, or hear what went on outside. The last evening we were out we went to see the family of the Collector of Excise, Mr Holmes. They were a large family; father, mother, grandmother, three or four sons, three daughters, and a little grandchild. We left them all well at 9 pm and next morning at nine o'clock we heard that Mr Holmes, his mother, two sons, a daughter and the little child were all dead and buried.

After that (which occurred the sixth day of the cholera) we stayed pretty much in the house. There was a constant fumigation kept up. Plates of salt on which vitriolic acid was poured from time to time were placed outside all the windows and doors. Every morning as soon as we awoke, a dose of whiskey thickened with ginger was given us all, in quantities according to our ages. Gradually the street in which we lived thinned out, as by twos and threes our dead neighbors were carried away. One morning (the ninth day) four were carried at once dead out of the opposite house. Our neighbours on both sides died. On one side a little girl called Mary Sheridan was left alone and sick, and we could hear her cries. I begged my mother's leave to help her, and she let me go, with many fears. Poor Mary died in my arms an hour after. I returned home and, being well fumigated, was not affected.

Some descriptions of provisions became almost impossible to get. Milk, most of all, as none of the country people could be induced to come near the doomed town. We had a cow, and many persons (ladies whom we did not know except by sight) used to come and beg a little milk for their young children. The jugs used to be left on the doorstep, filled, and taken away.

At night many tar barrels and other combustible matters used to be burned along the street to try to purify the air, and they had a weird, unearthly look, gleaming out in the darkness. The cholera carts and cots had bells, which added to the horror, and the coffin maker, a man named Young, used to knock on the doors to inquire if any coffins were wanted.

This was a climax hard to bear. Few nerves could stand it, and we asked Young to desist. But still he would come, and one day I told him that if he came again I would throw water on him. Next day he knocked as usual – and out went the full contents of a big jug on his head. The fellow shook himself, looked up at me with a diabolical grin, shook his fist and said, 'If you die in an hour you shall not have a coffin.'

'Thank you,' said I. 'In that case I shan't care.' He came no more.

Day by day went without any change. The plague was not stayed. Every morning at daybreak a cry used to go from room to room over the house, 'Is anyone dead?' But we were mercifully spared. In our whole lone street only Dr Little's family and our own remained without loss.

On some days the cholera was more fatal than on others, and on those days we could see a heavy sulphurous looking cloud hang low over the house, and we heard that birds were found dead on the shores of Lough Gill.

Early on the morning of the fourteenth day, my mother heard a great commotion among the poultry in the backyard, and on going out found several of them dead or dying. She came in and said it was time for us to go and pack up. So we put up a few things, sent the cow to a meadow in the neighborhood where there was water, begged the people near to milk her and make use of the milk, and at ten o'clock we (that is, my father, mother, two brothers, myself and a servant) started on the mail coach for Ballyshannon, where lived some of my father's friends who we were sure would receive us for a few days till we could get some place to live in.

It was a damp, drizzling morning, and we felt very miserable, as if we had a forewarning of what lay before us. All went well until we got within a mile of a village about four miles from Ballyshannon, when the coach was met and stopped by a mob of men armed with sticks, scythes and pitchforks. They were headed by a Dr John Shields, who was half-mad. He was the son of one of the first physicians and most respected men in the county, but he did not take after his father. The coach was stopped and we were ordered out, our luggage taken off, and no entreaties could prevail on those men to allow us to pass. Fear had maddened them. After a long parley and many threats of the vengeance of the law, the coach was allowed to proceed, and we were left on the roadside sitting on our trunks, cold, wet, hungry, and well-nigh hopeless. My father feared to leave us to go and seek assistance, but after about an hour and a half, we saw my uncle's carriage and a hack chaise coming towards us.

One of my cousins was in the carriage. The family had heard of our situation and he had come out to try and bring us in. An old servant of the family who had a livery stable had brought his chaise – for the sake of old times. We got into the carriages, but when we neared Ballyshannon found we would not be allowed to remain; all we could get leave to do was drive through the town. My uncle had an old friend, a Mrs Walker, in Donegal, about twenty miles further on, and he advised our going there and wrote to beg her to receive us for a little. So on we went, my mother and we children in the chaise, and my father, the servant and luggage in the open carriage.

It was now raining as if heaven and earth were coming together, and after driving for about ten miles, my father looked very ill. Our store of cholera medicines (without which no one moved a yard) was produced, but we had no vessel to mix them in, so one of the drivers ran to a cabin in the fields and begged the loan of a mug and a little water. The woman gave it, but on the mug being returned, she broke it into pieces, and when offered some money said if we left it on the road she would take it up after a while, but feared to touch anything from our hands.

My father's illness was not cholera but the result of cold, anxiety and exhaustion, and he was soon well enough to continue. We entered Donegal, but our arrival had been announced in some way and we found the square where we entered full of men howling like devils. In a trice ourselves and our luggage were taken, or rather torn from the carriages, the luggage was piled in the centre of the square, we placed on it, and a cry went out, 'Fire to burn the cholera people!' We thought our last hour had surely come, and sat as quiet as we could and tried to be resigned to our fate. Fortunately, the officer in command of the regiment quartered in the town was a man of promptitude and humanity. The barracks gate opened into the square, and in an incredibly short time he ordered out the troops, who surrounded us in a square and faced the mob on all sides with fixed bayonets.

We were now comparatively safe, but in what condition. Wet, cold, hungry, houseless, and surrounded by a howling multitude who would not even allow us to go on. Presently a meeting of the magistrates was held to decide on what was to be done with us, and (I regret to have to tell it of a minister of Christ) the bitterest and least merciful among them was the rector of the parish. In the meantime some kind person sent us out a large jug of hot tea and a loaf, which we thankfully received. It was all the food we had had that day.

The magistrates decided that we should not be allowed to pass, but be sent back by the way we came, escorted by the military to protect us from the fury of the mob. So our carriages were again packed, and back we went with our escort, who left us about seven miles on the road. We now held a council of war as to what was to be done, and the drivers advised that we should wait till dark, and they would drive us by a back way to our cousin's house in Ballyshannon, where we were sure of shelter if we could once get there.

They walked the horses and about ten at night we arrived without detection and were warmly received by our cousins. We were fed and our feet bathed, and beginning to feel quite comfortable, when there was a great uproar in the street and the voice of our old enemy, Dr John Shields, called for us to be brought out. But we now had the best of it, and our cousins refused to open the doors.

The noises continued, and presently the chief magistrate of the town and two doctors arrived, and civilly requested admittance. They were let in on promising to abstain from violence, and we had to submit to a medical examination. We were declared free from cholera so far, but the house was put into quarantine and no one let out for some days.

At the end of that time we were able to live in peace till the plague had abated and we could return to Sligo. There we found the streets grass-grown and five-eighths of the population dead. We had great reason to thank God who had spared us.

SHORT STORIES

As might be expected, 'Dracula's Guest' is Bram Stoker's best known short story, published by his widow Florence two years after Bram's death. It is now widely accepted that the story was originally written as the first chapter of *Dracula*, but was eliminated in the editing process due to the overall length of the novel.

Bram wrote almost fifty short stories, depending how we count the stories he adapted from his longer works of fiction – which include another section of *Dracula* adapted as a short story 'Jonathan Harker's Journal' and published in the *New Edition of The Cabinet of Irish Literature, Volume 3* (1903).

While under copyright, Bram Stoker's stories were published in three collections and individually in innumerable newspapers and periodicals. In the years since the works have been in the public domain, certain stories have been published frequently. Some have fallen into relative obscurity, but many can be found printed in John Edgar Browning's *The Forgotten Writing of Bram Stoker* and on bramstoker.org.

The four stories included here are fairly representative of Bram's work over the span of his career.

THE CRYSTAL CUP

First published in the September 1872 issue of London Society: An Illustrated Magazine of Light and Amusing Literature for Hours of Relaxation, W Clowes and Sons, London.

When reading this story, it is interesting to consider where the story fits in the context of Bram's life and to notice the obvious influences. Notably, 'The Crystal Cup' was Bram's first published story and the genesis of familiar themes of mystical dreams, love, sleep, death, and the supernatural – which are recurring in Bram's other fiction.

The story was published when he was twenty-five years old, but he may have been working on the story for years. A year earlier he had begun making the first entries in his literary commonplace book that Dr Elizabeth Miller and I co-edited for publication as *Bram Stoker's Lost Journal: The Dublin Years* (2012).

In 1872, Bram had graduated from Trinity College and was still working in Dublin Castle as a clerk in the Department of Registrar of Petty Sessions Clerks. Bram felt like trapped in his mundane job as a clerk, imprisoned by his father's mandate that Bram sacrifice his creative soul for the sake of a secure, respectable position. Like his older sister Matilda, Bram was an accomplished artist and would become a founding member of the Dublin Painting and Sketching Club two years after 'The Crystal Cup' was published.

Themes of mystical dreams, love, sleep, death, and the supernatural – familiar and recurring in Bram's other fiction have their genesis in 'The Crystal Cup'. The young artist in the story appears to reflect Bram's memories of himself as a sickly young boy in Clontarf and Artane, confined to his room, looking out his window to the sea, losing himself in the dreams he creates. And in reality, it must have seemed unfair to Bram that while he slaved away, trapped in the Castle, his sisters were planning their trip to Europe to finish their education by experiencing the arts.

I. The Dream-Birth

The blue waters touch the walls of the palace; I can hear their soft, lapping wash against the marble whenever I listen. Far out at sea I can see the waves glancing in the sunlight, ever-smiling, ever-glancing, ever-sunny. Happy waves! – Happy in your gladness, thrice happy that ye are free!

I rise from my work and spring up the wall till I reach the embrasure. I grasp the corner of the stonework and draw myself up till I crouch in the wide window. Sea, sea, out away as far as my vision extends. There I gaze till my eyes grow dim; and in the dimness of my eyes my spirit finds its sight. My soul flies on the wings of memory away beyond the blue, smiling sea-away beyond the glancing waves and the gleaming sails, to the land I call my home. As the minutes roll by, my actual eyesight seems to be restored, and I look round me in my old birth-house. The rude simplicity of the dwelling comes back to me as something new. There I see my old books and manuscripts and pictures, and there, away on their old shelves, high up above the door, I see my first rude efforts in art.

How poor they seem to me now! And yet, were I free, I would not give the smallest of them for all I now possess. Possess? How I dream.

The dream calls me back to waking life. I spring down from my window-seat and work away frantically, for every line I draw on paper, every new form that springs on the plaster, brings me nearer freedom. I will make a vase whose beauty will put to shame the glorious works of Greece in her golden prime! Surely a love like mine and a hope like mine must in time make some form of beauty spring to life! When He beholds it he will exclaim with rapture, and will order my instant freedom. I can forget my hate, and the deep debt of revenge which I owe him when I think of liberty-even from his hands. Ah! Then on the wings of the morning shall I fly beyond the sea to my home-her home-and clasp her to my arms, never more to be separated!

But, oh Spirit of Day! If she should be – No, no, I cannot think of it, or I shall go mad. Oh Time, Time! Maker and destroyer of men's fortunes, why hasten so fast for others whilst thou laggest so slowly for me? Even now my home may have become desolate, and she-my bride of an hour-may sleep calmly in the cold earth. Oh this suspense will drive me mad! Work, work! Freedom is before me; Aurora is the reward of my labour!

So I rush to my work; but to my brain and hand, heated alike, no fire or no strength descends. Half mad with despair, I beat myself against the walls of my prison, and then climb into the embrasure, and once more gaze upon the ocean, but find there no hope. And so I stay till night, casting its pall of blackness over nature, puts the possibility of effort away from me for yet another day.

So my days go on, and grow to weeks and months. So will they grow to years, should life so long remain an unwelcome guest within me; for what is man without hope? And is not hope nigh dead within this weary breast?

Last night, in my dreams, there came, like an inspiration from the Day-Spirit, a design for my vase.

All day my yearning for freedom – for Aurora, or news of her – had increased tenfold, and my heart and brain were on fire. Madly I beat myself, like a caged bird, against my prison-bars. Madly I leaped to my window-seat, and gazed with bursting eyeballs out on the free, open sea. And there I sat till my passion had worn itself out; and then I slept, and dreamed of thee, Aurora-of thee and freedom. In my ears I heard again the old song we used to sing together, when as children we wandered on the beach; when, as lovers, we saw the sun sink in the ocean, and I would see its glory doubled as it shone in thine eyes, and was mellowed against thy cheek; and when, as my bride, you clung to me as my arms went round you on that desert tongue of land whence rushed that band of sea-robbers that tore me away. Oh! How my heart curses those men-not men, but fiends! But one solitary gleam of joy remains from that dread encounter, – that my struggle stayed those hell-hounds, and that, ere I was stricken down, this right hand sent one of them to his home. My spirit rises as I think of that blow that saved thee from a life worse than death. With the thought I feel my cheeks burning, and my forehead swelling with mighty veins. My eyes burn, and I rush wildly round my prison-house, 'Oh! For one of my enemies, that I might dash out his brains against these marble walls, and trample his heart out as he lay before me!' These walls would spare him not. They are pitiless, alas! I know too well.

'Oh, cruel mockery of kindness, to make a palace a prison, and to taunt a captive's aching heart with forms of beauty and sculptured marble!' Wondrous, indeed, are these sculptured walls! Men call them passing fair; but oh, Aurora! With thy beauty ever before my eyes, what form that men call lovely can be fair to me? Like him who gazes sun-wards, and then sees no light on Earth, from the glory that dyes his iris, so thy beauty or its memory has turned the fairest things of earth to blackness and deformity.

In my dream last night, when in my ears came softly, like music stealing across the waters from afar, the old song we used to sing together, then to my brain, like a ray of light, came an idea whose grandeur for a moment struck me dumb. Before my eyes grew a vase of such beauty that I knew my hope was born to life, and that the Great Spirit had placed my foot on the ladder that leads from this my palace-dungeon to freedom and to thee. Today I have got a block of crystal – for only in such pellucid substance can I body forth my dream – and have commenced my work.

I found at first that my hand had lost its cunning, and I was beginning to despair, when, like the memory of a dream, there came back in my ears the strains of the old song. I sang it softly to myself, and as I did so I grew calmer; but oh! How differently the song sounded to me when thy voice, Aurora, rose not in unison with my own! But what avails pining? To work! To work! Every touch of my chisel will bring me nearer thee.

My vase is daily growing nearer to completion. I sing as I work, and my constant song is the one I love so well. I can hear the echo of my voice in the vase; and as I end, the wailing song note is prolonged in sweet, sad music in the crystal cup. I listen, ear down, and sometimes I weep as I listen, so sadly comes the echo to my song. Imperfect though it be, my voice makes sweet music, and its echo in the cup guides my hand towards perfection as I work. Would that thy voice rose and fell with mine, Aurora, and then the world would behold a vase of such beauty as never before woke up the slumbering fires of mans love for what is fair; for if I do such work in sadness, imperfect as I am in my solitude and sorrow, what would I do in joy, perfect when with thee? I know that my work is good as an artist, and I feel that it is as a man; and the cup itself, as it daily grows in beauty, gives back a clearer echo. Oh! If I worked in joy how gladly would it give back our voices! Then would we hear an echo and music such as mortals seldom hear; but now the echo, like my song, seems imperfect. I grow daily weaker; but still I work on-work with my whole soul – for am I not working for freedom and for thee?

My work is nearly done. Day by day, hour by hour, the vase grows more finished. Ever clearer comes the echo whilst I sing; ever softer, ever more sad and heart-rending comes the echo of the wail at the end of the song. Day by day I grow weaker and weaker; still I work on with all my soul. At night the thought comes to me, whilst I think of thee, that I will never see thee more – that I breathe out my life into the crystal cup, and that it will last there when I am gone.

So beautiful has it become, so much do I love it, that I could gladly die to be maker of such a work, were it not for thee – for my love for thee, and my hope of thee, and my fear for thee, and my anguish for thy grief when thou knowest I am gone.

My work requires but few more touches. My life is slowly ebbing away, and I feel that with my last touch my life will pass out for ever into the cup. Till that touch is given I must not die – I will not die. My hate has passed away. So great are my wrongs that revenge of mine would be too small a compensation for my woe. I leave revenge to a juster and a mightier than I. Thee, oh Aurora, I will await in the land of flowers, where thou and I will wander, never more to part, never more! Ah, never more! Farewell, Aurora – Aurora – Aurora!

II. The Feast of Beauty

The Feast of Beauty approaches rapidly, yet hardly so fast as my royal master wishes. He seems to have no other thought than to have this feast greater and better than any ever held before. Five summers ago his Feast of Beauty was nobler than all held in his sires reign together; yet scarcely was it over, and the rewards given to the victors, when he conceived the giant project whose success is to be tested when the moon reaches her full. It was boldly chosen and boldly done; chosen and done as boldly as the project of a monarch should be. But still I cannot think that it will end well. This yearning after completeness must be unsatisfied in the end-this desire that makes a monarch fling his kingly justice to the winds, and strive to reach his Mecca over a desert of blighted hopes and lost lives. But hush! I must not dare to think ill of my master or his deeds; and besides, walls have ears. I must leave alone these dangerous topics, and confine my thoughts within proper bounds.

The moon is waxing quickly, and with its fulness comes the Feast of Beauty, whose success as a whole rests almost solely on my watchfulness and care; for if the ruler of the feast should fail in his duty, who could fill the void? Let me see what arts are represented, and what works compete. All the arts will have trophies: poetry in its various forms, and prose-writing; sculpture with carving in various metals, and glass, and wood, and ivory, and engraving gems, and setting jewels; painting on canvas, and glass, and wood, and stone and metal; music, vocal and instrumental; and dancing. If that woman will but sing, we will have a real triumph of music; but she appears sickly too. All our best artists either get ill or die, although we promise them freedom or rewards or both if they succeed.

Surely never yet was a Feast of Beauty so fair or so richly dowered as this which the full moon shall behold and hear; but ah! The crowning glory of the feast will be the crystal cup. Never yet have these eyes beheld such a form of beauty, such a wondrous mingling of substance and light. Surely some magic power must have helped to draw such loveliness from a cold block of crystal. I must be careful that no harm happens the vase. Today when I touched it, it gave forth such a ringing sound that my heart jumped with fear lest it should sustain any injury. Henceforth, till I deliver it up to my master, no hand but my own shall touch it lest any harm should happen to it.

Strange story has that cup. Born to life in the cell of a captive torn from his artist home beyond the sea, to enhance the splendour of a feast by his labour-seen at work by spies, and traced and followed till a chance – cruel chance for him – gave him into the hands of the emissaries of my master. He too, poor moth, fluttered about the flame: the name of freedom spurred him on to exertion till he wore away his life. The beauty of that cup was dearly bought for him. Many a man would forget his captivity whilst he worked at such a piece of loveliness; but he appeared to have some sorrow at his heart, some sorrow so great that it quenched his pride.

How he used to rave at first! How he used to rush about his chamber, and then climb into the embrasure of his window, and gaze out away over the sea! Poor captive! Perhaps over the sea some one waited for his coming who was dearer to him than many cups, even many cups as beautiful as this, if such could be on Earth ... Well, well, we must all die soon or late, and who dies first escapes the more sorrow, perhaps, who knows? How, when he had commenced the cup, he used to sing all day long, from the moment the sun shot its first fiery arrow into the retreating hosts of night-clouds, till the shades of evening advancing drove the lingering sunbeams into the west-and always the same song!

How he used to sing, all alone! Yet sometimes I could almost imagine I heard not one voice from his chamber, but two ... No more will it echo again from the wall of a dungeon, or from a hillside in free air. No more will his eyes behold the beauty of his crystal cup.

It was well he lived to finish it. Often and often have I trembled to think of his death, as I saw him day by day grow weaker as he worked at the unfinished vase. Must his eyes never more behold the beauty that was born of his soul? Oh, never more! Oh Death, grim King of Terrors, how mighty is thy sceptre! All-powerful is the wave of thy hand that summons us in turn to thy kingdom away beyond the poles!

Would that thou, poor captive, hadst lived to behold thy triumph, for victory will be thine at the Feast of Beauty such as man never before achieved. Then thou mightst have heard the shout that hails the victor in the contest, and the plaudits that greet him as he passes out, a free man, through the palace gates. But now thy cup will come to light amid the smiles of beauty and rank and power, whilst thou liest there in thy lonely chamber, cold as the marble of its walls.

And, after all, the feast will be imperfect, since the victors cannot all be crowned. I must ask my master's direction as to how a blank place of a competitor, should he prove a victor, is to be filled up. So late? I must see him ere the noontide hour of rest be past.

Great Spirit! How I trembled as my master answered my question!

I found him in his chamber, as usual in the noontide. He was lying on his couch disrobed, half-sleeping; and the drowsy zephyr, scented with rich odours from the garden, wafted through the windows at either side by the fans, lulled him to complete repose. The darkened chamber was cool and silent. From the vestibule came the murmuring of many fountains, and the pleasant splash of falling waters. 'Oh, happy,' said I, in my heart, 'oh, happy great King, that has such pleasures to enjoy!' The breeze from the fans swept over the strings of the æolian harps, and a sweet, confused, happy melody arose like the murmuring of children's voices singing afar off in the valleys, and floating on the wind.

As I entered the chamber softly, with muffled foot-fall and pent-in breath, I felt a kind of awe stealing over me. To me who was born and have dwelt all my life within the precincts of the court-to me who talk daily with my royal master, and take his minutest directions as to the coming feast-to me who had all my life looked up to my king as to a spirit, and had venerated him as more than mortal – came a feeling of almost horror; for my master looked then, in his quiet chamber, half-sleeping amid the drowsy music of the harps and fountains, more like a common man than a God. As the thought came to me I shuddered in affright, for it seemed to me that I had been guilty of sacrilege. So much had my veneration for my royal master become a part of my nature, that but to think of him as another man seemed like the anarchy of my own soul.

I came beside the couch, and watched him in silence. He seemed to be half-listening to the fitful music; and as the melody swelled and died away his chest rose and fell as he breathed in unison with the sound.

After a moment or two he appeared to become conscious of the presence of some one in the room, although by no motion of his face could I see that he heard any sound, and his eyes were shut. He opened his eyes, and, seeing me, asked, 'Was all right about the Feast of Beauty?' for that is the subject ever nearest to his thoughts. I answered that all was well, but that I had come to ask his royal pleasure as to how a vacant place amongst the competitors was to be filled up. He asked, 'How vacant?' and on my telling him, 'from death,' he asked again, quickly, 'Was the work finished?' When I told him that it was, he lay back again on his couch with a sigh of relief, for he had half arisen in his anxiety as he asked the question. Then he said, after a minute, 'All the competitors must be present at the feast.' 'All?' said I. 'All,' he answered again, 'alive or dead; for the old custom must be preserved, and the victors crowned.' He stayed still for a minute more, and then said, slowly, 'Victors or martyrs.' And I could see that the kingly spirit was coming back to him.

Again he went on. 'This will be my last Feast of Beauty; and all the captives shall be set free. Too much sorrow has sprung already from my ambition. Too much injustice has soiled the name of king.'

He said no more, but lay still and closed his eyes. I could see by the working of his hands and the heaving of his chest that some violent emotion troubled him, and the thought arose, 'He is a man, but he is yet a king; and, though a king as he is, still happiness is not for him. Great Spirit of Justice! Thou metest out his pleasures and his woes to man, to king and slave alike! Thou lovest best to whom thou givest peace!'

Gradually my master grew more calm, and at length sunk into a gentle slumber; but even in his sleep he breathed in unison with the swelling murmur of the harps.

'To each is given,' said I gently, 'something in common with the world of actual things. Thy life, oh King, is bound by chains of sympathy to the voice of Truth, which is Music! Tremble, lest in the presence of a master-strain thou shouldst feel thy littleness, and die!' and I softly left the room.

III. The Story of the Moonbeam

Slowly I creep along the bosom of the waters.

Sometimes I look back as I rise upon a billow, and see behind me many of my kin sitting each upon a wave-summit as upon a throne. So I go on for long, a power that I wist not forcing me onward, without will or purpose of mine.

At length, as I rise upon a mimic wave, I see afar a hazy light that springs from a vast palace, through whose countless windows flame lamps and torches. But at the first view, as if my coming had been the signal, the lights disappear in an instant.

Impatiently I await what may happen; and as I rise with each heart-beat of the sea, I look forward to where the torches had gleamed. Can it be a deed of darkness that shuns the light?

The time has come when I can behold the palace without waiting to mount upon the waves. It is built of white marble, and rises steep from the brine. Its sea-front is glorious with columns and statues; and from the portals the marble steps sweep down, broad and wide to the waters, and below them, down as deep as I can see.

No sound is heard, no light is seen. A solemn silence abounds, a perfect calm.

Slowly I climb the palace walls, my brethren following as soldiers up a breach. I slide along the roofs, and as I look behind me walls and roofs are glistening as with silver. At length I meet with something smooth and hard and translucent; but through it I pass and enter a vast hall, where for an instant I hang in mid-air and wonder.

My coming has been the signal for such a burst of harmony as brings back to my memory the music of the spheres as they rush through space; and in the full-swelling anthem of welcome I feel that I am indeed a sun-spirit, a child of light, and that this is homage to my master.

I look upon the face of a great monarch, who sits at the head of a banquet-table. He has turned his head upwards and backwards, and looks as if he had been awaiting my approach. He rises and fronts me with the ringing out of the welcome-song, and all the others in the great hall turn towards me as well. I can see their eyes gleaming. Down along the immense table, laden with plate and glass and flowers, they stand holding each a cup of ruby wine, with which they pledge the monarch when the song is ended, as they drink success to him and to the 'Feast of Beauty'.

I survey the hall. An immense chamber, with marble walls covered with bas-reliefs and frescoes and sculptured figures, and panelled by great columns that rise along the surface and support a dome-ceiling painted wondrously; in its centre the glass lantern by which I entered.

On the walls are hung pictures of various forms and sizes, and down the centre of the table stretches a raised platform on which are placed works of art of various kinds.

At one side of the hall is a dais on which sit persons of both sexes with noble faces and lordly brows, but all wearing the same expression-care tempered by hope. All these hold scrolls in their hands.

At the other side of the hall is a similar dais, on which sit others fairer to earthly view, less spiritual and more marked by surface-passion. They hold music-scores. All these look more joyous than those on the other platform, all save one, a woman, who sits with downcast face and dejected mien, as of one without hope. As my light falls at her feet she looks up, and I feel happy. The sympathy between us has called a faint gleam of hope to cheer that poor pale face.

Many are the forms of art that rise above the banquet-table, and all are lovely to behold. I look on all with pleasure one by one, till I see the last of them at the end of the table away from the monarch, and then all the others seem as nothing to me. What is this that makes other forms of beauty seem as nought when compared with it, when brought within the radius of its lustre? A crystal cup, wrought with such wondrous skill that light seems to lose its individual glory as it shines upon it and is merged in its beauty. 'Oh Universal Mother, let me enter there. Let my life be merged in its beauty, and no more will I regret my sun-strength hidden deep in the chasms of my moon-mother. Let me live there and perish there, and I will be joyous whilst it lasts, and content to pass into the great vortex of nothingness to be born again when the glory of the cup has fled.'

Can it be that my wish is granted, that I have entered the cup and become a part of its beauty? 'Great Mother, I thank thee.'

Has the cup life? Or is it merely its wondrous perfectness that makes it tremble, like a beating heart, in unison with the ebb and flow, the great wave-pulse of nature? To me it feels as if it had life.

I look through the crystal walls and see at the end of the table, isolated from all others, the figure of a man seated. Are those cords that bind his limbs? How suits that crown of laurel those wide, dim eyes, and that pallid hue? It is passing strange. This Feast of Beauty holds some dread secrets, and sees some wondrous sights.

I hear a voice of strange, rich sweetness, yet wavering-the voice of one almost a king by nature. He is standing up; I see him through my palace-wall. He calls a name and sits down again.

Again I hear a voice from the platform of scrolls, the Throne of Brows; and again I look and behold a man who stands trembling yet flushed, as though the morning light shone bright upon his soul. He reads in cadenced measure a song in praise of my moon-mother, the Feast of Beauty, and the king. As he speaks, he trembles no more, but seems inspired, and his voice rises to a tone of power and grandeur, and rings back from walls and dome. I hear his words distinctly, though saddened in tone, in the echo from my crystal home. He concludes and sits down, half-fainting, amid a whirlwind of applause, every note, every beat of which is echoed as the words had been.

Again the monarch rises and calls 'Aurora,' that she may sing for freedom. The name echoes in the cup with a sweet, sad sound. So sad, so despairing seems the echo, that the hall seems to darken and the scene to grow dim.

'Can a sun-spirit mourn, or a crystal vessel weep?'

She, the dejected one, rises from her seat on the Throne of Sound, and all eyes turn upon her save those of the pale one, laurel-crowned. Thrice she essays to begin, and thrice nought comes from her lips but a dry, husky sigh, till an old man who has been moving round the hall settling all things, cries out, in fear lest she should fail, 'Freedom!'

The word is re-echoed from the cup. She hears the sound, turns towards it and begins.

Oh, the melody of that voice! And yet it is not perfect alone; for after the first note comes an echo from the cup that swells in unison with the voice, and the two sounds together, seem as if one strain came ringing sweet from the lips of the All-Father himself. So sweet it is, that all throughout the hall sit spell-bound, and scarcely dare to breathe.

In the pause after the first verses of the song, I hear the voice of the old man speaking to a comrade, but his words are unheard by any other, 'Look at the king. His spirit seems lost in a trance of melody. Ah! I fear me some evil: the nearer the music approaches to perfection the more rapt he becomes. I dread lest a perfect note shall prove his death-call.' His voice dies away as the singer commences the last verse.

Sad and plaintive is the song; full of feeling and tender love, but love overshadowed by grief and despair. As it goes on the voice of the singer grows sweeter and more thrilling, more real; and the cup, my crystal time-home, vibrates more and more as it gives back the echo. The monarch looks like one entranced, and no movement is within the hall … The song dies away in a wild wail that seems to tear the heart of the singer in twain; and the cup vibrates still more as it gives back the echo. As the note, long-swelling, reaches its highest, the cup, the Crystal Cup, my wondrous home, the gift of the All-

Father, shivers into millions of atoms, and passes away.

Ere I am lost in the great vortex I see the singer throw up her arms and fall, freed at last, and the King sitting, glory-faced, but pallid with the hue of Death.

THE SQUAW

'The Squaw' by Bram Stoker originally published in the 2 December, 1893 issue of *Holly Leaves: the Christmas Number of The Illustrated Sporting and Dramatic News*, London.

I feel strongly that feeling that this story has an autobiographical flavour to it. It was in Bram's nature to write what he knew – stories based on some version of real places, events and people – especially his own adventures – as in the case of 'The Squaw'. However, Bram was adept at writing vivid descriptions of scenes he had never experienced first-hand and that could be the case with Nuremberg.

In 1882 and in again in 1895, to prepare for staging *Faust*, Irving traveled to Nuremberg and Rothenberg with others from the Lyceum to get a feel for the local flavour, which was especially important for the scene painters. It's quite possible that Bram was with the group in 1882, but not likely in 1895. Bram and Florence travelled to Germany other times and occasions but for example, I can't verify how many times they attended the Bayreuth Festival (according to Bram, 1902 and according to another writer, 1901) or how many other trips might have been inspired by Bram's friendship with the festival's house conductor, Hans Richter or Florence's love of musical theatre.

Perhaps Bram (and Florence) did see the Iron Maiden in Nuremberg before 'The Squaw' was published in 1890. But an 1893 news article detailed recent history of the 'famous torture instruments from the Royal Castle of Nuremberg' which since being sold in 1890 have 'been exhibited in London and elsewhere throughout the Kingdom of Great Britain with much success'. Which would have been a 'must see' for Bram Stoker.

My first foray into the world of graphic novels was with *The Virgin's Embrace* (2021), a StokerVerse™ graphic novel that Dr Chris McAuley and I adapted from 'The Squaw'.

Nurnberg at the time was not so much exploited as it has been since then. Irving had not been playing *Faust*, and the very name of the old town was hardly known to the great bulk of the travelling public. My wife and I being in the second week of our honeymoon, naturally wanted someone else to join our party, so that when the cheery stranger, Elias P Hutcheson, hailing from Isthmian City, Bleeding Gulch, Maple Tree County, Neb turned up at the station at Frankfort, and casually remarked that he was going on to see the most all-fired old Methuselah of a town in Yurrup, and that he guessed that so much travelling alone was enough to send an intelligent, active citizen into the melancholy ward of a daft house, we took the pretty broad hint and suggested that we should join forces. We found, on comparing notes afterwards, that we had each intended to speak with some diffidence or hesitation so as not to appear too eager, such not being a good compliment to the success of our married life; but the effect was entirely marred by our both beginning to speak at the same instant – stopping simultaneously and then going on together again. Anyhow, no matter how, it was done; and Elias P Hutcheson became one of our party. Straightway Amelia and I found the pleasant benefit; instead of quarrelling, as we had been doing, we found that the restraining influence of a third party was such that we now took every opportunity of spooning in odd corners. Amelia declares that ever since she has, as the result of that experience, advised all her friends to take a friend on the honeymoon. Well, we 'did' Nurnberg together, and much enjoyed the racy remarks of our Transatlantic friend, who, from his quaint speech and his wonderful stock of adventures, might have stepped out of a novel. We kept for the last object of interest in the city to be visited the Burg, and on the day appointed for the visit strolled round the outer wall of the city by the eastern side.

The Burg is seated on a rock dominating the town and an immensely deep fosse guards it on the northern side. Nurnberg has been happy in that it was never sacked; had it been it would certainly not be so spick and span perfect as it is at present. The ditch has not been used for centuries, and now its base is spread with tea-gardens and orchards, of which some of the trees are of quite respectable growth. As we wandered round the wall, dawdling in the hot July sunshine, we often paused to admire the views spread before us, and in especial the great plain covered with towns and villages and bounded with a blue line of hills, like a landscape of Claude Lorraine. From this we always turned with new delight to the city itself, with its myriad of quaint old gables and acre-wide red roofs dotted with dormer windows, tier upon tier. A little to our right rose the towers of the Burg, and nearer still, standing grim, the Torture Tower, which was, and is, perhaps, the most interesting place in the city. For centuries the tradition of the Iron Virgin of Nurnberg has been handed down as an instance of the horrors of cruelty of which man is capable; we had long looked forward to seeing it; and here at last was its home.

In one of our pauses we leaned over the wall of the moat and looked down. The garden seemed quite fifty or sixty feet below us, and the sun pouring into it with an intense, moveless heat like that of an oven. Beyond rose the grey, grim wall seemingly of endless height, and losing itself right and left in the angles of bastion and counterscarp. Trees and bushes crowned the wall, and above again towered the lofty houses on whose massive beauty Time has only set the hand of approval. The sun was hot and we were lazy; time was our own, and we lingered, leaning on the wall. Just below us was a pretty sight – a great black cat lying stretched in the sun, whilst round her gambolled prettily a tiny black kitten. The mother would wave her tail for the kitten to play with, or would raise her feet and push away the little one as an encouragement to further play. They were just at the foot of the wall, and Elias P Hutcheson, in order to help the play, stooped and took from the walk a moderate sized pebble.

'See!' he said, 'I will drop it near the kitten, and they will both wonder where it came from.'

'Oh, be careful,' said my wife; 'you might hit the dear little thing!'

'Not me, ma'am,' said Elias P. 'Why, I'm as tender as a Maine cherry-tree. Lor, bless ye. I wouldn't hurt the poor pooty little critter more'n I'd scalp a baby. An' you may bet your variegated socks on that! See, I'll drop it fur away on the outside so's not to go near her!' Thus saying, he leaned over and held his arm out at full length and dropped the stone. It may be that there is some attractive force which draws lesser matters to greater; or more probably that the wall was not plump but sloped to its base—we not noticing the inclination from above; but the stone fell with a sickening thud that came up to us through the hot air, right on the kitten's head, and shattered out its little brains then and there. The black cat cast a swift upward glance, and we saw her eyes like green fire fixed an instant on Elias P Hutcheson; and then her attention was given to the kitten, which lay still with just a quiver of her tiny limbs, whilst a thin red stream trickled from a gaping wound. With a muffled cry, such as a human being might give, she bent over the kitten licking its wounds and moaning. Suddenly she seemed to realise that it was dead, and again threw her eyes up at us. I shall never forget the sight, for she looked the perfect incarnation of hate. Her green eyes blazed with lurid fire, and the white, sharp teeth seemed to almost shine through the blood which dabbled her mouth and whiskers. She gnashed her teeth, and her claws stood out stark and at full length on every paw. Then she made a wild rush up the wall as if to reach us, but when the momentum ended fell back, and further added to her horrible appearance for she fell on the kitten, and rose with her black fur smeared with its brains and blood. Amelia turned quite faint, and I had to lift her back from the wall. There was a seat close by in shade of a spreading plane-tree, and here I placed her whilst she composed herself. Then I went back to Hutcheson, who stood without moving, looking down on the angry cat below.

As I joined him, he said:

'Wall, I guess that air the savagest beast I ever see – 'cept once when an Apache squaw had an edge on a half-breed what they nicknamed "Splinters" 'cos of the way he fixed up her papoose which he stole on a raid just to show that he appreciated the way they had given his mother the fire torture. She got that kinder look so set on her face that it jest seemed to grow there. She followed Splinters mor'n three year till at last the braves got him and handed him over to her. They did say that no man, white or Injun, had ever been so long a-dying under the tortures of the Apaches. The only time I ever see her smile was when I wiped her out. I kem on the camp just in time to see Splinters pass in his checks, and he wasn't sorry to go either. He was a hard citizen, and though I never could shake with him after that papoose business – for it was bitter bad, and he should have been a white man, for he looked like one – I see he had got paid out in full. Durn me, but I took a piece of his hide from one of his skinnin' posts an' had it made into a pocket-book. It's here now!' and he slapped the breast pocket of his coat.

Whilst he was speaking the cat was continuing her frantic efforts to get up the wall. She would take a run back and then charge up, sometimes reaching an incredible height. She did not seem to mind the heavy fall which she got each time but started with renewed vigour; and at every tumble her appearance became more horrible. Hutcheson was a kind-hearted man – my wife and I had both noticed little acts of kindness to animals as well as to persons – and he seemed concerned at the state of fury to which the cat had wrought herself.

'Wall, now!' he said, 'I du declare that that poor critter seems quite desperate. There! There! Poor thing, it was all an accident – though that won't bring back your little one to you. Say! I wouldn't have had such a thing happen for a thousand! Just shows what a clumsy fool of a man can do when he tries to play! Seems I'm too darned slipperhanded to even play with a cat. Say Colonel!' – it was a pleasant way he had to bestow titles freely – 'I hope your wife don't hold no grudge against me on account of this unpleasantness? Why, I wouldn't have had it occur on no account.'

He came over to Amelia and apologised profusely, and she with her usual kindness of heart hastened to assure him that she quite understood that it was an accident. Then we all went again to the wall and looked over.

The cat, missing Hutcheson's face, had drawn back across the moat, and was sitting on her haunches as though ready to spring. Indeed, the very instant she saw him she did spring, and with a blind unreasoning fury, which would have been grotesque, only that it was so frightfully real. She did not try to run up the wall, but simply launched herself at him as though hate and fury could lend her wings to pass straight through the great distance between them. Amelia, womanlike, got quite concerned, and said to Elias P in a warning voice:

'Oh! You must be very careful. That animal would try to kill you if she were here; her eyes look like positive murder.'

He laughed out jovially. 'Excuse me, ma'am,' he said, 'but I can't help laughin'. Fancy a man that has fought grizzlies an' Injuns bein' careful of bein' murdered by a cat!'

When the cat heard him laugh, her whole demeanour seemed to change. She no longer tried to jump or run up the wall, but went quietly over, and sitting again beside the dead kitten began to lick and fondle it as though it were alive.

'See!' said I, 'the effect of a really strong man. Even that animal in the midst of her fury recognises the voice of a master, and bows to him!'

'Like a squaw!' was the only comment of Elias P Hutcheson, as we moved on our way round the city fosse. Every now and then we looked over the wall and each time saw the cat following us. At first she had kept going back to the dead kitten, and then as the distance grew greater took it in her mouth and so followed. After a while, however, she abandoned this, for we saw her following all alone; she had evidently hidden the body somewhere. Amelia's alarm grew at the cat's persistence, and more than once she repeated her warning; but the American always laughed with amusement, till finally, seeing that she was beginning to be worried, he said:

'I say, ma'am, you needn't be skeered over that cat. I go heeled, I du!' Here he slapped his pistol pocket at the back of his lumbar region. 'Why sooner'n have you worried, I'll shoot the critter, right here, an' risk the police interferin' with a citizen of the United States for carryin' arms contrairy to reg'lations!' As he spoke he looked over the wall, but the cat, on seeing him, retreated, with a growl, into a bed of tall flowers, and was hidden. He went on: 'Blest if that ar critter ain't got more sense of what's good for her than most Christians. I guess we've seen the last of her! You bet, she'll go back now to that busted kitten and have a private funeral of it, all to herself!'

Amelia did not like to say more, lest he might, in mistaken kindness to her, fulfil his threat of shooting the cat: and so we went on and crossed the little wooden bridge leading to the gateway whence ran the steep paved roadway between the Burg and the pentagonal Torture Tower. As we crossed the bridge we saw the cat again down below us. When she saw us her fury seemed to return, and she made frantic efforts to get up the steep wall. Hutcheson laughed as he looked down at her, and said:

'Goodbye, old girl. Sorry I injured your feelin's, but you'll get over it in time! So long!' And then we passed through the long, dim archway and came to the gate of the Burg.

When we came out again after our survey of this most beautiful old place which not even the well-intentioned efforts of the Gothic restorers of forty years ago have been able to spoil – though their restoration was then glaring white – we seemed to have quite forgotten the unpleasant episode of the morning. The old lime tree with its great trunk gnarled with the passing of nearly nine centuries, the deep well cut through the heart of the rock by those captives of old, and the lovely view from the city wall whence we heard, spread over almost a full quarter of an hour, the multitudinous chimes of the city, had all helped to wipe out from our minds the incident of the slain kitten.

We were the only visitors who had entered the Torture Tower that morning – so at least said the old custodian – and as we had the place all to ourselves were able to make a minute and more satisfactory survey than would have otherwise been possible. The custodian, looking to us as the sole source of his gains for the day, was willing to meet our wishes in any way. The Torture Tower is truly a grim place, even now when many thousands of visitors have sent a stream of life, and the joy that follows life, into the place; but at the time I mention it wore its grimmest and most gruesome aspect. The dust of ages seemed to have settled on it, and the darkness and the horror of its memories seem to have become sentient in a way that would have satisfied the Pantheistic souls of Philo or Spinoza. The lower chamber where we entered was seemingly, in its normal state, filled with incarnate darkness; even the hot sunlight streaming in through the door seemed to be lost in the vast thickness of the walls, and only showed the masonry rough as when the builder's scaffolding had come down, but coated with dust and marked here and there with patches of dark stain which, if walls could speak, could have given their own dread memories of fear and pain. We were glad to pass up the dusty wooden staircase, the custodian leaving the outer door open to light us somewhat on our way; for to our eyes the one long-wick'd, evil-smelling candle stuck in a sconce on the wall gave an inadequate light. When we came up through the open trap in the corner of the chamber overhead, Amelia held on to me so tightly that I could actually feel her heart beat. I must say for my own part that I was not surprised at her fear, for this room was even more gruesome than that below. Here there was certainly more light, but only just sufficient to realise the horrible surroundings of the place. The builders of the tower had evidently intended that only they who should gain the top should have any of the joys of light and prospect. There, as we had noticed from below, were ranges of windows, albeit of mediaeval smallness, but elsewhere in the tower were only a very few narrow slits such as were habitual in places of mediaeval defence. A few of these only lit the chamber, and these so high up in the wall that from no part could the sky be seen through the thickness of the walls. In racks, and leaning in disorder against the walls, were a number of headsmen's swords, great double-handed weapons with broad blade and keen edge. Hard by were several blocks whereon the necks of the victims had lain, with here and there deep notches where the steel had bitten through the guard of flesh and shored into the wood. Round the chamber, placed in all sorts of irregular ways, were many implements of torture which made one's heart ache to see – chairs full of spikes which gave instant and excruciating pain; chairs and couches with dull knobs whose torture was seemingly less, but which, though slower, were equally efficacious; racks, belts, boots, gloves, collars, all made for compressing at will; steel baskets in which the head could be slowly crushed into a pulp if necessary; watchmen's hooks with long handle and knife that cut at resistance – this a speciality of the old Nurnberg police system; and many, many other devices for man's injury to man. Amelia grew quite pale with the horror of the things, but fortunately did not faint, for being a little overcome she sat down on a torture chair, but jumped up again with a shriek, all tendency to faint gone. We both pretended that it was the injury done to her dress by the dust of the chair, and the rusty spikes which had upset her, and Mr Hutcheson acquiesced in accepting the explanation with a kind-hearted laugh.

But the central object in the whole of this chamber of horrors was the engine known as the Iron Virgin, which stood near the centre of the room. It was a rudely-shaped figure of a woman, something of the bell order, or, to make a closer comparison, of the figure of Mrs Noah in the children's Ark, but without that slimness of waist and perfect *rondeur* of hip which marks the aesthetic type of the Noah family. One would hardly have recognised it as intended for a human figure at all had not the founder shaped on the forehead a rude semblance of a woman's face. This machine was coated with rust without, and covered with dust; a rope was fastened to a ring in the front of the figure, about where the waist should have been, and was drawn through a pulley, fastened on the wooden pillar which sustained the flooring above. The custodian pulling this rope showed that a section of the front was hinged like a door at one side; we then saw that the engine was of considerable thickness, leaving just room enough inside for a man to be placed. The door was of equal thickness and of great weight, for it took the custodian all his strength, aided though he was by the contrivance of the pulley, to open it. This weight was partly due to the fact that the door was of manifest purpose hung so as to throw its weight downwards, so that it might shut of its own accord when the strain was released. The inside was honeycombed with rust—nay more, the rust alone that comes through time would hardly have eaten so deep into the iron walls; the rust of the cruel stains was deep indeed! It was only, however, when we came to look at the inside of the door that the diabolical intention was manifest to the full. Here were several long spikes, square and massive, broad at the base and sharp at the points, placed in such a position that when the door should close the upper ones would pierce the eyes of the victim, and the lower ones his heart and vitals. The sight was too much for poor Amelia, and this time she fainted dead off, and I had to carry her down the stairs, and place her on a bench outside till she recovered. That she felt it to the quick was afterwards shown by the fact that my eldest son bears to this day a rude birthmark on his breast, which has, by family consent, been accepted as representing the Nurnberg Virgin.

When we got back to the chamber we found Hutcheson still opposite the Iron Virgin; he had been evidently philosophising, and now gave us the benefit of his thought in the shape of a sort of exordium.

'Wall, I guess I've been learnin' somethin' here while madam has been gettin' over her faint. 'Pears to me that we're a long way behind the times on our side of the big drink. We uster think out on the plains that the Injun could give us points in tryin' to make a man uncomfortable; but I guess your old mediaeval law-and-order party could raise him every time. Splinters was pretty good in his bluff on the squaw, but this here young miss held a straight flush all high on him. The points of them spikes air sharp enough still, though even the edges air eaten out by what uster be on them. It'd be a good thing for our Indian section to get some specimens of this here play-toy to send round to the Reservations jest to knock the stuffin' out of the bucks, and the squaws too, by showing them as how old civilisation lays over them at their best. Guess but I'll get in that box a minute jest to see how it feels!'

'Oh no! no!' said Amelia. 'It is too terrible!'

'Guess, ma'am, nothin's too terrible to the explorin' mind. I've been in some queer places in my time. Spent a night inside a dead horse while a prairie fire swept over me in Montana Territory – an' another time slept inside a dead buffler when the Comanches was on the war path an' I didn't keer to leave my kyard on them. I've been two days in a caved-in tunnel in the Billy Broncho gold mine in New Mexico, an' was one of the four shut up for three parts of a day in the caisson what slid over on her side when we was settin' the foundations of the Buffalo Bridge. I've not funked an odd experience yet, an' I don't propose to begin now!'

We saw that he was set on the experiment, so I said: 'Well, hurry up, old man, and get through it quick!'

'All right, General,' said he, 'but I calculate we ain't quite ready yet. The gentlemen, my predecessors, what stood in that thar canister, didn't volunteer for the office – not much! And I guess there was some ornamental tyin' up before the big stroke was made. I want to go into this thing fair and square, so I must get fixed up proper first. I dare say this old galoot can rise some string and tie me up accordin' to sample?'

This was said interrogatively to the old custodian, but the latter, who understood the drift of his speech, though perhaps not appreciating to the full the niceties of dialect and imagery, shook his head. His protest was, however, only formal and made to be overcome. The American thrust a gold piece into his hand, saying: 'Take it, pard! It's your pot; and don't be skeer'd. This ain't no necktie party that you're asked to assist in!' He produced some thin frayed rope and proceeded to bind our companion with sufficient strictness for the purpose. When the upper part of his body was bound, Hutcheson said:

'Hold on a moment, Judge. Guess I'm too heavy for you to tote into the canister. You jest let me walk in, and then you can wash up regardin' my legs!'

Whilst speaking he had backed himself into the opening which was just enough to hold him. It was a close fit and no mistake. Amelia looked on with fear in her eyes, but she evidently did not like to say anything. Then the custodian completed his task by tying the American's feet together so that he was now absolutely helpless and fixed in his voluntary prison. He seemed to really enjoy it, and the incipient smile which was habitual to his face blossomed into actuality as he said:

'Guess this here Eve was made out of the rib of a dwarf! There ain't much room for a full-grown citizen of the United States to hustle. We uster make our coffins more roomier in Idaho territory. Now, Judge, you jest begin to let this door down, slow, on to me. I want to feel the same pleasure as the other jays had when those spikes began to move toward their eyes!'

'Oh no! no! no!' broke in Amelia hysterically. 'It is too terrible! I can't bear to see it! – I can't! I can't!' But the American was obdurate. 'Say, Colonel,' said he, 'why not take Madame for a little promenade? I wouldn't hurt her feelin's for the world; but now that I am here, havin' kem eight thousand miles, wouldn't it be too hard to give up the very experience I've been pinin' an' pantin' fur? A man can't get to feel like canned goods every time! Me and the Judge here'll fix up this thing in no time, an' then you'll come back, an' we'll all laugh together!'

Once more the resolution that is born of curiosity triumphed, and Amelia stayed holding tight to my arm and shivering whilst the custodian began to slacken slowly inch by inch the rope that held back the iron door. Hutcheson's face was positively radiant as his eyes followed the first movement of the spikes.

'Wall!' he said, 'I guess I've not had enjoyment like this since I left Noo York. Bar a scrap with a French sailor at Wapping – an' that warn't much of a picnic neither – I've not had a show fur real pleasure in this dod-rotted Continent, where there ain't no b'ars nor no Injuns, an' wheer nary man goes heeled. Slow there, Judge! Don't you rush this business! I want a show for my money this game – I du!'

The custodian must have had in him some of the blood of his predecessors in that ghastly tower, for he worked the engine with a deliberate and excruciating slowness which after five minutes, in which the outer edge of the door had not moved half as many inches, began to overcome Amelia. I saw her lips whiten, and felt her hold upon my arm relax. I looked around an instant for a place whereon to lay her, and when I looked at her again found that her eye had become fixed on the side of the Virgin. Following its direction I saw the black cat crouching out of sight. Her green eyes shone like danger lamps in the gloom of the place, and their colour was heightened by the blood which still smeared her coat and reddened her mouth. I cried out:

'The cat! look out for the cat!' for even then she sprang out before the engine. At this moment she looked like a triumphant demon. Her eyes blazed with ferocity, her hair bristled out till she seemed twice her normal size, and her tail lashed about as does a tiger's when the quarry is before it. Elias P Hutcheson when he saw her was amused, and his eyes positively sparkled with fun as he said:

'Darned if the squaw hain't got on all her war paint! Jest give her a shove off if she comes any of her tricks on me, for I'm so fixed everlastingly by the boss, that durn my skin if I can keep my eyes from her if she wants them! Easy there, Judge! don't you slack that ar rope or I'm euchered!'

At this moment Amelia completed her faint, and I had to clutch hold of her round the waist or she would have fallen to the floor. Whilst attending to her I saw the black cat crouching for a spring, and jumped up to turn the creature out.

But at that instant, with a sort of hellish scream, she hurled herself, not as we expected at Hutcheson, but straight at the face of the custodian. Her claws seemed to be tearing wildly as one sees in the Chinese drawings of the dragon rampant, and as I looked I saw one of them light on the poor man's eye, and actually tear through it and down his cheek, leaving a wide band of red where the blood seemed to spurt from every vein.

With a yell of sheer terror which came quicker than even his sense of pain, the man leaped back, dropping as he did so the rope which held back the iron door. I jumped for it, but was too late, for the cord ran like lightning through the pulley-block, and the heavy mass fell forward from its own weight.

As the door closed I caught a glimpse of our poor companion's face. He seemed frozen with terror. His eyes stared with a horrible anguish as if dazed, and no sound came from his lips.

And then the spikes did their work. Happily the end was quick, for when I wrenched open the door they had pierced so deep that they had locked in the bones of the skull through which they had crushed, and actually tore him – it – out of his iron prison till, bound as he was, he fell at full length with a sickly thud upon the floor, the face turning upward as he fell.

I rushed to my wife, lifted her up and carried her out, for I feared for her very reason if she should wake from her faint to such a scene. I laid her on the bench outside and ran back. Leaning against the wooden column was the custodian moaning in pain whilst he held his reddening handkerchief to his eyes. And sitting on the head of the poor American was the cat, purring loudly as she licked the blood which trickled through the gashed socket of his eyes.

I think no one will call me cruel because I seized one of the old executioner's swords and shore her in two as she sat.

THE SEER

'The Seer', being Chapters 1 and 2 of *The Mystery of the Sea* (1902) may have been published in this abbreviated form in a newspaper or periodical while still under copyright. *The Mystery of the Sea*, in its entirety, was serialised in the *Denver Post* in 1904 and possibly in other papers or periodicals.

There is some question regarding the first two chapters of *The Mystery of the Sea* and whether Bram did in fact publish it as a short story, entitled 'The Seer'. Although I am not yet convinced that he did, I include it here to introduce readers to *The Mystery of the Sea*.

Bram went first to Port Erroll (now known as Cruden Bay) in 1892 in hope of finding a quiet seaside location to enjoy a summer holiday with his wife and son and to escape London & the stresses of managing the Lyceum Theatre. Cruden Bay turned out to be the perfect location where he could relax and write, much like Whitby, Yorkshire in many ways, except far less commercial. Bram would spend twelve summers in Cruden Bay and recreate the area in two of his novels, *The Watters Mou'*, and *The Mystery of the Sea*. And it was while staying in Cruden Bay and nearby Whinnyfold that Bram wrote large portions of *Dracula*. The villagers had endless stories to share with Bram – religious, historical and superstitious – some with the Doric dialect he would recreate so faithfully when writing.

Bram was very open-minded and interested in the occult, mesmerism, and spiritualism; he was fascinated by the 'fair folks', superstitions and social rituals that dictated the lives of the fearless souls living in this somewhat isolated area. 'The Seer' introduces the 'Bram-like' character, Archibald Hunter, and Gormala MacNiel, an old woman and a seer, who understands that Archibald also possesses the ability of second sight. Hunter is very much like Bram himself, and while standing with local author, guide and friend, Mike Shepherd on the bridge in front of the Kilmarnock Arms Hotel – which is the exact spot where Archibald meets Gormala – I could almost feel the blurred lines between reality and imagination in Bram Stoker's world.

CHAPTER I
SECOND SIGHT

I had just arrived at Cruden Bay on my annual visit, and after a late breakfast was sitting on the low wall which was a continuation of the escarpment of the bridge over the Water of Cruden. Opposite to me, across the road and standing under the only little clump of trees in the place was a tall, gaunt old woman, who kept looking at me intently. As I sat, a little group, consisting of a man and two women, went by. I found my eyes follow them, for it seemed to me after they had passed me that the two women walked together and the man alone in front carrying on his shoulder a little black box – a coffin. I shuddered as I thought, but a moment later I saw all three abreast just as they had been. The old woman was now looking at me with eyes that blazed. She came across the road and said to me without preface:

'What saw ye then, that yer e'en looked so awed?' I did not like to tell her so I did not answer. Her great eyes were fixed keenly upon me, seeming to look me through and through. I felt that I grew quite red, whereupon she said, apparently to herself: 'I thocht so! Even I did not see that which he saw.'

'How do you mean?' I queried.

She answered ambiguously: 'Wait! Ye shall perhaps know before this hour to-morrow!'

Her answer interested me and I tried to get her to say more; but she would not. She moved away with a grand statcly movement that seemed to become her great gaunt form.

After dinner whilst I was sitting in front of the hotel, there was a great commotion in the village; much running to and fro of men and women with sad mien. On questioning them I found that a child had been drowned in the little harbour below. Just then a woman and a man, the same that had passed the bridge earlier in the day, ran by with wild looks. One of the bystanders looked after them pityingly as he said:

'Puir souls. It's a sad home-comin' for them the nicht.'

'Who are they?' I asked. The man took off his cap reverently as he answered:

'The father and mother of the child that was drowned!' As he spoke I looked round as though some one had called me.

There stood the gaunt woman with a look of triumph on her face.

The curved shore of Cruden Bay, Aberdeenshire, is backed by a waste of sandhills in whose hollows seagrass and moss and wild violets, together with the pretty 'grass of Parnassus' form a green carpet. The surface of the hills is held together by bent-grass and is eternally shifting as the wind takes the fine sand and drifts it to and fro. All behind is green, from the meadows that mark the southern edge of the bay to the swelling uplands that stretch away and away far in the distance, till the blue mist of the mountains at Braemar sets a kind of barrier. In the centre of the bay the highest point of the land that runs downward to the sea looks like a miniature hill known as the Hawklaw; from this point onward to the extreme south, the land runs high with a gentle trend downwards.

Cruden sands are wide and firm and the sea runs out a considerable distance. When there is a storm with the wind on shore the whole bay is a mass of leaping waves and broken water that threatens every instant to annihilate the stake-nets which stretch out here and there along the shore. More than a few vessels have been lost on these wide stretching sands, and it was perhaps the roaring of the shallow seas and the terror which they inspired which sent the crews to the spirit room and the bodies of those of them which came to shore later on, to the churchyard on the hill.

If Cruden Bay is to be taken figuratively as a mouth, with the sand hills for soft palate, and the green Hawklaw as the tongue, the rocks which work the extremities are its teeth. To the north the rocks of red granite rise jagged and broken. To the south, a mile and a half away as the crow flies, Nature seems to have manifested its wildest forces. It is here, where the little promontory called Whinnyfold juts out, that the two great geological features of the Aberdeen coast meet. The red sienite of the north joins the black gneiss of the south. That union must have been originally a wild one; there are evidences of an upheaval which must have shaken the earth to its centre. Here and there are great masses of either species of rock hurled upwards in every conceivable variety of form, sometimes fused or pressed together so that it is impossible to say exactly where gneiss ends or sienite begins; but broadly speaking here is an irregular line of separation. This line runs seawards to the east and its strength is shown in its outcrop. For half a mile or more the rocks rise through the sea singly or in broken masses ending in a dangerous cluster known as 'The Skares' and which has had for centuries its full toll of wreck and disaster. Did the sea hold its dead where they fell, its floor around the Skares would be whitened with their bones, and new islands could build themselves with the piling wreckage. At times one may see here the ocean in her fiercest mood; for it is when the tempest drives from the south-east that the sea is fretted amongst the rugged rocks and sends its spume landwards. The rocks that at calmer times rise dark from the briny deep are lost to sight for moments in the grand onrush of the waves. The seagulls which usually whiten them, now flutter around screaming, and the sound of their shrieks comes in on the gale almost in a continuous note, for the single cries are merged in the multitudinous roar of sea and air.

The village, squatted beside the emboucher of the Water of Cruden at the northern side of the bay is simple enough; a few rows of fishermen's cottages, two or three great red-tiled drying-sheds nestled in the sand-heap behind the fishers' houses. For the rest of the place as it was when first I saw it, a little lookout beside a tall flagstaff on the northern cliff, a few scattered farms over the inland prospect, one little hotel down on the western bank of the Water of Cruden with a fringe of willows protecting its sunk garden which was always full of fruits and flowers.

From the most southern part of the beach of Cruden Bay to Whinnyfold village the distance is but a few hundred yards; first a steep pull up the face of the rock; and then an even way, beside part of which runs a tiny stream. To the left of this path, going towards Whinnyfold, the ground rises in a bold slope and then falls again all round, forming a sort of wide miniature hill of some eighteen or twenty acres. Of this the southern side is sheer, the black rock dipping into the waters of the little bay of Whinnyfold, in the centre of which is a picturesque island of rock shelving steeply from the water on the northern side, as is the tendency of all the gneiss and granite in this part. But to east and north there are irregular bays or openings, so that the furthest points of the promontory stretch out like fingers. At the tips of these are reefs of sunken rock falling down to deep water and whose existence can only be suspected in bad weather when the rush of the current beneath sends up swirling eddies or curling masses of foam. These little bays are mostly curved and are green where falling earth or drifting sand have hidden the outmost side of the rocks and given a foothold to the seagrass and clover. Here have been at some time or other great caves, now either fallen in or silted up with sand, or obliterated with the earth brought down in the rush of surface-water in times of long rain. In one of these bays, Broad Haven, facing right out to the Skares, stands an isolated pillar of rock called locally the 'Puir mon' through whose base, time and weather have worn a hole through which one may walk dryshod.

Through the masses of rocks that run down to the sea from the sides and shores of all these bays are here and there natural channels with straight edges as though cut on purpose for the taking in of the cobbles belonging to the fisher folk of Whinnyfold.

When first I saw the place I fell in love with it. Had it been possible I should have spent my summer there, in a house of my own, but the want of any place in which to live forbade such an opportunity. So I stayed in the little hotel, the Kilmarnock Arms.

The next year I came again, and the next, and the next. And then I arranged to take a feu at Whinnyfold and to build a house overlooking the Skares for myself. The details of this kept me constantly going to Whinnyfold, and my house to be was always in my thoughts.

Hitherto my life had been an uneventful one. At school I was, though secretly ambitious, dull as to results. At College I was better off, for my big body and athletic powers gave me a certain position in which I had to overcome my natural shyness. When I was about eight and twenty I found myself nominally a barrister, with no knowledge whatever of the practice of law and but little less of the theory, and with a commission in the Devil's Own – the irreverent name given to the Inns of Court Volunteers. I had few relatives, but a comfortable, though not great, fortune; and I had been round the world, dilettante fashion.

CHAPTER II
GORMALA

All that night I thought of the dead child and of the peculiar vision which had come to me. Sleeping or waking it was all the same; my mind could not leave the parents in procession as seen in imagination, or their distracted mien in reality. Mingled with them was the great-eyed, aquiline-featured, gaunt old woman who had taken such an interest in the affair, and in my part of it. I asked the landlord if he knew her, since, from his position as postmaster he knew almost everyone for miles around. He told me that she was a stranger to the place. Then he added:

'I can't imagine what brings her here. She has come over from Peterhead two or three times lately; but she doesn't seem to have anything at all to do. She has nothing to sell and she buys nothing. She's not a tripper, and she's not a beggar, and she's not a thief, and she's not a worker of any sort. She's a queer-looking lot anyhow. I fancy from her speech that she's from the west; probably from some of the far-out islands. I can tell that she has the Gaelic from the way she speaks.'

Later on in the day, when I was walking on the shore near the Hawklaw, she came up to speak to me. The shore was quite lonely, for in those days it was rare to see anyone on the beach except when the salmon fishers drew their nets at the ebbing tide. I was walking towards Whinnyfold when she came upon me silently from behind. She must have been hidden among the bent-grass of the sandhills for had she been anywhere in view I must have seen her on that desolate shore. She was evidently a most imperious person; she at once addressed me in a tone and manner which made me feel as though I were in some way an inferior, and in somehow to blame:

'What for did ye no tell me what ye saw yesterday?' Instinctively I answered:

'I don't know why. Perhaps because it seemed so ridiculous.' Her stern features hardened into scorn as she replied:

'Are Death and the Doom then so redeekulous that they pleasure ye intil silence?' I somehow felt that this was a little too much and was about to make a sharp answer, when suddenly it struck me as a remarkable thing that she knew already. Filled with surprise I straightway asked her:

'Why, how on earth do you know? I told no one.' I stopped for I felt all at sea; there was some mystery here which I could not fathom. She seemed to read my mind like an open book, for she went on looking at me as she spoke, searchingly and with an odd smile.

'Eh! laddie, do ye no ken that ye hae een that can see? Do ye no understand that ye hae een that can speak? Is it that one with the Gift o' Second Sight has no an understandin' o' it. Why, yer face when ye saw the mark o' the Doom, was like a printed book to een like mine.'

'Do you mean to tell me,' I asked 'that you could tell what I saw, simply by looking at my face?'

'Na! na! laddie. Not all that, though a Seer am I; but I knew that you had seen the Doom! It's no that varied that there need be any mistake. After all Death is only one, in whatever way we may speak!' After a pause of thought I asked her:

'If you have the power of Second Sight why did you not see the vision, or whatever it was, yourself?'

'Eh! Laddie' she answered, shaking her head ''Tis little ye ken o' the wark o' the Fates! Learn ye then that the Voice speaks only as it listeth into chosen ears, and the Vision comes only to chosen een. None can will to hear or to see, to pleasure themselves.'

'Then,' I said, and I felt that there was a measure of triumph in my tone, 'if to none but the chosen is given to know, how comes it that you, who seem not to have been chosen on this occasion at all events, know all the same?' She answered with a touch of impatience:

'Do ye ken, young sir, that even mortal een have power to see much, if there be behind them the thocht, an' the knowledge and the experience to guide them aright. How, think ye, is it that some can see much, and learn much as they gang; while others go blind as the mowdiwart, at the end o' the journey as before it?'

'Then perhaps you will tell me how much you saw, and how you saw it?'

'Ah! To them that have seen the Doom there needs but sma' guidance to their thochts. Too lang, an' too often hae I mysen seen the death-sark an' the watch-candle an' the dead-hole, not to know when they are seen tae ither een. Na, na! Laddie, what I kent o' yer seein' was no by the Gift but only by the use o' my proper een. I kent not the muckle o' what ye saw. Not whether it was ane or ither o' the garnishins o' the dead; but weel I kent that it was o' death.'

'Then,' I said interrogatively, 'Second Sight is altogether a matter of chance?'

'Chance! Chance!' she repeated with scorn. 'Na! Young sir; when the Voice has spoken there is no more chance than that the nicht will follow the day.'

'You mistake me,' I said, feeling somewhat superior now that I had caught her in an error. 'I did not for a moment mean that the Doom – whatever it is – is not a true forerunner. What I meant was that it seems to be a matter of chance in whose ear the Voice – whatever it is – speaks; when once it has been ordained that it is to sound in the ear of some one.' Again she answered with scorn:

'Na, na! There is no chance o' ocht aboot the Doom. Them that send forth the Voice and the Seein' know well to whom it is sent and why. Can ye no comprehend that it is for no bairn-play that such goes forth. When the Voice speaks, it is mainly followed by tears an' woe an' lamentation! Nae! Nor is it only one bit manifestation that stands by its lanes, remote and isolate from all ither. Truly 'tis but a pairt o' the great scheme o' things; an' be sure that whoso is chosen to see or to hear is chosen weel, an' must hae their pairt in what is to be, on to the verra end.'

'Am I to take it,' I asked, 'that Second Sight is but a little bit of some great purpose which has to be wrought out by means of many kinds; and that whoso sees the Vision or hears the Voice is but the blind unconscious instrument of Fate?'

'Aye! Laddie. Weel eneuch the Fates know their wishes an' their wark, no to need the help or the thocht of any human – blind or seein', sane or silly, conscious or unconscious.'

All through her speaking I had been struck by the old woman's use of the word 'Fate', and more especially when she used it in the plural. It was evident that, Christian though she might be – and in the West they are generally devout observants of the duties of their creed – her belief in this respect came from some of the old pagan mythologies. I should have liked to question her on this point; but I feared to shut her lips against me. Instead I asked her:

'Tell me, will you, if you don't mind, of some case you have known yourself of Second Sight?'

''Tis no for them to brag or boast to whom has been given to see the wark o' the hand o' Fate. But sine ye are yerself a Seer an' would learn, then I may speak. I hae seen the sea ruffle wi'oot cause in the verra spot where later a boat was to gang doon, I hae heard on a lone moor the hammerin' o' the coffin-wright when one passed me who was soon to dee. I hae seen the death-sark fold round the speerit o' a drowned one, in baith ma sleepin' an' ma wakin' dreams. I hae heard the settin' doom o' the Spaiks, an' I hae seen the Weepers on a' the crood that walked. Aye, an' in mony anither way hae I seen an' heard the Coming o' the Doom.'

'But did all the seeings and hearings come true?' I asked. 'Did it ever happen that you heard queer sounds or saw strange sights and that yet nothing came of them? I gather that you do not always know to whom something is going to happen; but only that death is coming to some one!' She was not displeased at my questioning but replied at once:

'Na doot! But there are times when what is seen or heard has no manifest following. But think ye, young sir, how mony a corp, still waited for, lies in the depths o' the sea; how mony lie oot on the hillsides, or are fallen in deep places where their bones whiten unkent. Nay! More, to how many has Death come in a way that men think the wark o' nature when his hastening has come frae the hand of man, untold.' This was a difficult matter to answer so I changed or rather varied the subject.

'How long must elapse before the warning comes true?'

'Ye know yersel', for but yestreen ye hae seen, how the Death can follow hard upon the Doom; but there be times, nay mostly are they so, when days or weeks pass away ere the Doom is fulfilled.'

'Is this so,' I asked, 'when you know the person regarding whom the Doom is spoken?' She answered with an air of certainty which somehow carried conviction, secretly, with it.

'Even so! I know one who walks the airth now in all the pride o' his strength. But the Doom has been spoken of him. I saw him with these verra een lie prone on rocks, wi' the water rinnin' down from his hair. An' again I heard the minute bells as he went by me on a road where is no bell for a score o' miles. Aye, an' yet again I saw him in the kirk itsel' wi' corbies flyin' round him, an' mair gatherin' from afar!'

Here was indeed a case where Second Sight might be tested; so I asked her at once, though to do so I had to overcome a strange sort of repugnance:

'Could this be proved? Would it not be a splendid case to make known; so that if the death happened it would prove beyond all doubt the existence of such a thing as Second Sight.' My suggestion was not well received. She answered with slow scorn:

'Beyon' all doot! Doot! Wha is there that doots the bein' o' the Doom? Learn ye too, young sir, that the Doom an' all thereby is no for traffickin' wi' them that only cares for curiosity and publeecity.

The Voice and the Vision o' the Seer is no for fine madams and idle gentles to while away their time in play-toy make-believe!' I climbed down at once.

'Pardon me!' I said. 'I spoke without thinking. I should not have said so – to you at any rate.' She accepted my apology with a sort of regal inclination; but the moment after she showed by her words she was after all but a woman!

'I will tell ye; that so in the full time ye may hae no doot yersel'. For ye are a Seer and as Them that has the power hae gien ye the Gift it is no for the like o' me to cumber the road o' their doin'. Know ye then, and remember weel, how it was told ye by Gormala MacNiel that Lauchlane Macleod o' the Outer Isles hae been Called; tho' as yet the Voice has no sounded in his ears but only in mine. But ye will see the time –'

She stopped suddenly as though some thought had struck her, and then went on impressively:

'When I saw him lie prone on the rocks there was ane that bent ower him that I kent not in the nicht wha it was, though the licht o' the moon was around him. We shall see! We shall see!'

Without a word more she turned and left me. She would not listen to my calling after her; but with long strides passed up the beach and was lost among the sandhills.

THE JUDGE'S HOUSE

First published in *Holly Leaves: the Christmas Number of The Illustrated Sporting and Dramatic News*, 5 December, 1891, London; and in book form in *Dracula's Guest And Other Weird Stories* (1914) George Routledge & Sons, Ltd., London.

At the time 'The Judge's House' was published in 1891, Bram had published five short stories and his first novel, *The Snake's Pass*. He had begun researching *Dracula* in 1890 while living in London and working as the acting manager of the Lyceum Theatre. His career was in full swing – as Henry Irving's right hand man – writing short stories and novels in his free time.

For the 'The Judge's House' Bram drew on his experiences as a student at Trinity College and working in Dublin Castle as a Clerk of Petty Sessions. The central character, Malcom, a young college student, bears a certain resemblance to Bram who received a MA in Math from Trinity College Dublin in 1875. Bram used to take the train from Dublin south to the end of the line to a town called Greystones, where he could get away from the hustle and bustle of Dublin. Greystones, like Malcom's Benchurch, was a place for Bram to relax and focus on writing or possibly like Malcom Malcolmson, study for his examinations in Mathematics.

With Bram's legal background, first as a clerk, then as the Inspector of Clerks of Petty Sessions throughout Ireland, he would have been aware of the reputations of the two infamous hanging judges: the Welshman Lord George Jeffreys (1645-1689) and the Irishman John Toler, Earl of Norbury (1745-1831), either of whom was a perfect model for the owner of the Judge's House.

'The Judge's House' is often considered one of Bram's best pieces of short fiction, relying on one of the familiar themes of *Dracula*: the lone man in a castle-like structure, trying to make sense of the rooms and the situation in which he finds himself. See if you agree …

When the time for his examination drew near Malcolm Malcolmson made up his mind to go somewhere to read by himself. He feared the attractions of the seaside, and also he feared completely rural isolation, for of old he knew its charms, and so he determined to find some unpretentious little town where there would be nothing to distract him. He refrained from asking suggestions from any of his friends, for he argued that each would recommend some place of which he had knowledge, and where he had already acquaintances. As Malcolmson wished to avoid friends he had no wish to encumber himself with the attention or friends' friends, and so he determined to look out for a place for himself. He packed a portmanteau with some clothes and all the books he required, and then took ticket for the first name on the local time-table which he did not know.

When at the end of three hours' journey he alighted at Benchurch, he felt satisfied that he had so far obliterated his tracks as to be sure of having a peaceful opportunity of pursuing his studies. He went straight to the one inn which the sleepy little place contained, and put up for the night. Benchurch was a market town, and once in three weeks was crowded to excess, but for the remainder of the twenty-one days it was as attractive as a desert. Malcolmson looked around the day after his arrival to try to find quarters more isolated than even so quiet an inn as 'The Good Traveller' afforded. There was only one place which took his fancy, and it certainly satisfied his wildest ideas regarding quiet; in fact, quiet was not the proper word to apply to it – desolation was the only term conveying any suitable idea of its isolation. It was an old rambling, heavy-built house of the Jacobean style, with heavy gables and windows, unusually small, and set higher than was customary in such houses, and was surrounded with a high brick wall massively built. Indeed, on examination, it looked more like a fortified house than an ordinary dwelling. But all these things pleased Malcolmson. 'Here,' he thought, 'is the very spot I have been looking for, and if I can only get opportunity of using it I shall be happy.' His joy was increased when he realised beyond doubt that it was not at present inhabited.

From the post-office he got the name of the agent, who was rarely surprised at the application to rent a part of the old house. Mr Carnford, the local lawyer and agent, was a genial old gentleman, and frankly confessed his delight at anyone being willing to live in the house.

'To tell you the truth,' said he, 'I should be only too happy, on behalf of the owners, to let anyone have the house rent free for a term of years if only to accustom the people here to see it inhabited. It has been so long empty that some kind of absurd prejudice has grown up about it, and this can be best put down by its occupation – if only,' he added with a sly glance at Malcomson, 'by a scholar like yourself, who wants its quiet for a time.'

Malcolmson thought it needless to ask the agent about the 'absurd prejudice'; he knew he would get more information, if he should require it, on that subject from other quarters. He paid his three months' rent, got a receipt, and the name of an old woman who would probably undertake to 'do' for him, and came away with the keys in his pocket. He then went to the landlady of the inn, who was a cheerful and most kindly person, and asked her advice as to such stores and provisions as he would be likely to require. She threw up her hands in amazement when he told her where he was going to settle himself.

'Not in the Judge's House!' she said, and grew pale as she spoke. He explained the locality of the house, saying that he did not know its name. When he had finished she answered:

'Aye, sure enough – sure enough the very place! It is the Judge's House sure enough.' He asked her to tell him about the place, why so called, and what there was against it. She told him that it was so called locally because it had been many years before – how long she could not say, as she was herself from another part of the country, but she thought it must have been a hundred years or more – the abode of a judge who was held in great terror on account of his harsh sentences and his hostility to prisoners at Assizes. As to what there was against the house itself she could not tell. She had often asked, but no one could inform her; but there was a general feeling that there was something, and for her own part she would not take all the money in Drinkwater's Bank and stay in the house an hour by herself. Then she apologised to Malcolmson for her disturbing talk.

'It is too bad of me, sir, and you – and a young gentleman, too – if you will pardon me saying it, going to live there all alone. If you were my boy – and you'll excuse me for saying it – you wouldn't sleep there a night, not if I had to go there myself and pull the big alarm bell that's on the roof!' The good creature was so manifestly in earnest, and was so kindly in her intentions, that Malcolmson, although amused, was touched. He told her kindly how much he appreciated her interest in him, and added:

'But, my dear Mrs Witham, indeed you need not be concerned about me! A man who is reading for the Mathematical Tripos has too much to think of to be disturbed by any of these mysterious "somethings", and his work is of too exact and prosaic a kind to allow of his having any corner in his mind for mysteries of any kind. Harmonical Progression, Permutations and Combinations, and Elliptic Functions have sufficient mysteries for me!' Mrs Witham kindly undertook to see after his commissions, and he went himself to look for the old woman who had been recommended to him. When he returned to the Judge's House with her, after an interval of a couple of hours, he found Mrs Witham herself waiting with several men and boys carrying parcels, and an upholsterer's man with a bed in a cart, for she said, though tables and chairs might be all very well, a bed that hadn't been aired for mayhap fifty years was not proper for young bones to lie on. She was evidently curious to see the inside of the house; and though manifestly so afraid of the 'somethings' that at the slightest sound she clutched on to Malcolmson, whom she never left for a moment, went over the whole place.

After his examination of the house, Malcolmson decided to take up his abode in the great dining-room, which was big enough to serve for all his requirements; and Mrs Witham, with the aid of the charwoman, Mrs Dempster, proceeded to arrange matters. When the hampers were brought in and unpacked, Malcolmson saw that with much kind forethought she had sent from her own kitchen sufficient provisions to last for a few days. Before going she expressed all sorts of kind wishes; and at the door turned and said:

'And perhaps, sir, as the room is big and draughty it might be well to have one of those big screens put round your bed at night – though, truth to tell, I would die myself if I were to be so shut in with all kinds of – of "things", that put their heads round the sides, or over the top, and look on me!' The image which she had called up was too much for her nerves, and she fled incontinently.

Mrs Dempster sniffed in a superior manner as the landlady disappeared, and remarked that for her own part she wasn't afraid of all the bogies in the kingdom.

'I'll tell you what it is, sir,' she said; 'bogies is all kinds and sorts of things – except bogies! Rats and mice, and beetles; and creaky doors, and loose slates, and broken panes, and stiff drawer handles, that stay out when you pull them and then fall down in the middle of the night. Look at the wainscot of the room! It is old – hundreds of years old! Do you think there's no rats and beetles there! And do you imagine, sir, that you won't see none of them! Rats is bogies, I tell you, and bogies is rats; and don't you get to think anything else!'

'Mrs Dempster,' said Malcolmson gravely, making her a polite bow, 'you know more than a Senior Wrangler! And let me say, that, as a mark of esteem for your indubitable soundness of head and heart, I shall, when I go, give you possession of this house, and let you stay here by yourself for the last two months of my tenancy, for four weeks will serve my purpose.'

'Thank you kindly, sir!' she answered, 'but I couldn't sleep away from home a night. I am in Greenhow's Charity, and if I slept a night away from my rooms I should lose all I have got to live on. The rules is very strict; and there's too many watching for a vacancy for me to run any risks in the matter. Only for that, sir, I'd gladly come here and attend on you altogether during your stay.'

'My good woman,' said Malcolmson hastily, 'I have come here on purpose to obtain solitude; and believe me that I am grateful to the late Greenhow for having so organised his admirable charity – whatever it is – that I am perforce denied the opportunity of suffering from such a form of temptation! Saint Anthony himself could not be more rigid on the point!'

The old woman laughed harshly. 'Ah, you young gentlemen,' she said, 'you don't fear for naught; and belike you'll get all the solitude you want here.' She set to work with her cleaning; and by nightfall, when Malcolmson returned from his walk – he always had one of his books to study as he walked – he found the room swept and tidied, a fire burning in the old hearth, the lamp lit, and the table spread for supper with Mrs Witham's excellent fare. 'This is comfort, indeed,' he said, as he rubbed his hands. When he had finished his supper, and lifted the tray to the other end of the great oak dining-table, he got out his books again, put fresh wood on the fire, trimmed his lamp, and set himself down to a spell of real hard work. He went on without pause till about eleven o'clock, when he knocked off for a bit to fix his fire and lamp, and to make himself a cup of tea. He had always been a tea-drinker, and during his college life had sat late at work and had taken tea late. The rest was a great luxury to him, and he enjoyed it with a sense of delicious, voluptuous ease. The renewed fire leaped and sparkled, and threw quaint shadows through the great old room; and as he sipped his hot tea he revelled in the sense of isolation from his kind. Then it was that he began to notice for the first time what a noise the rats were making.

'Surely,' he thought, 'they cannot have been at it all the time I was reading. Had they been. I must have noticed it!' Presently, when the noise increased, he satisfied himself that it was really new. It was evident that at first the rats had been frightened at the presence of a stranger, and the light of fire and lamp; but that as the time went on they had grown bolder and were now disporting themselves as was their wont.

How busy they were! And hark to the strange noises! Up and down behind the old wainscot, over the ceiling and under the floor they raced, and gnawed, and scratched! Malcolmson smiled to himself as he recalled to mind the saying of Mrs Dempster, 'Bogies is rats, and rats is bogies!' The tea began to have its effect of intellectual and nervous stimulus, he saw with joy another long spell of work to be done before the night was past, and in the sense of security which it gave him, he allowed himself the luxury of a good look round the room. He took his lamp in one hand, and went all around, wondering that so quaint and beautiful an old house had been so long neglected. The carving of the oak on the panels of the wainscot was fine, and on and round the doors and windows it was beautiful and of rare merit. There were some old pictures on the walls, but they were coated so thick with dust and dirt that he could not distinguish any detail of them, though he held his lamp as high as he could over his head. Here and there as he went round he saw some crack or hole blocked for a moment by the face of a rat with its bright eyes glittering in the light, but in an instant it was gone, and a squeak and a scamper followed.

The thing that most struck him, however, was the rope of the great alarm bell on the roof, which hung down in a corner of the room on the right-hand side of the fireplace. He pulled up close to the hearth a great high-backed carved oak chair, and sat down to his last cup of tea. When this was done he made up the fire, and went back to his work, sitting at the corner of the table, having the fire to his left. For a while the rats disturbed him somewhat with their perpetual scampering, but he got accustomed to the noise as one does to the ticking of a clock or to the roar of moving water; and he became so immersed in his work that everything in the world, except the problem which he was trying to solve, passed away from him.

He suddenly looked up, his problem was still unsolved, and there was in the air that sense of the hour before the dawn, which is so dread to doubtful life. The noise of the rats had ceased. Indeed it seemed to him that it must have ceased but lately and that it was the sudden cessation which had disturbed him. The fire had fallen low, but still it threw out a deep red glow. As he looked he started in spite of his sang froid.

There on the great high-backed carved oak chair by the right side of the fireplace sat an enormous rat, steadily glaring at him with baleful eyes. He made a motion to it as though to hunt it away, but it did not stir. Then he made the motion of throwing something. Still it did not stir, but showed its great white teeth angrily, and its cruel eyes shone in the lamplight with an added vindictiveness.

Malcolmson felt amazed, and seizing the poker from the hearth ran at it to kill it. Before, however, he could strike it, the rat, with a squeak that sounded like the concentration of hate, jumped upon the floor, and, running up the rope of the alarm bell, disappeared in the darkness beyond the range of the green-shaded lamp. Instantly, strange to say, the noisy scampering of the rats in the wainscot began again.

By this time Malcolmson's mind was quite off the problem; and as a shrill cock-crow outside told him of the approach of morning, he went to bed and to sleep.

He slept so sound that he was not even waked by Mrs Dempster coming in to make up his room. It was only when she had tidied up the place and got his breakfast ready and tapped on the screen which closed in his bed that he woke. He was a little tired still after his night's hard work, but a strong cup of tea soon freshened him up, and, taking his book, he went out for his morning walk, bringing with him a few sandwiches lest he should not care to return till dinner time. He found a quiet walk between high elms some way outside the town, and here he spent the greater part of the day studying his Laplace. On his return he looked in to see Mrs Witham and to thank her for her kindness. When she saw him coming through the diamond-paned bay-window of her sanctum she came out to meet him and asked him in. She looked at him searchingly and shook her head as she said:

'You must not overdo it, sir. You are paler this morning than you should be. Too late hours and too hard work on the brain isn't good for any man! But tell me, sir, how did you pass the night? Well, I hope? But, my heart! Sir, I was glad when Mrs Dempster told me this morning that you were all right and sleeping sound when she went in.'

'Oh, I was all right,' he answered, smiling, 'the "somethings" didn't worry me, as yet. Only the rats; and they had a circus, I tell you, all over the place. There was one wicked looking old devil that sat up on my own chair by the fire, and wouldn't go till I took the poker to him, and then he ran up the rope of the alarm bell and got to somewhere up the wall or the ceiling – I couldn't see where, it was so dark.'

'Mercy on us,' said Mrs Witham, 'an old devil, and sitting on a chair by the fireside! Take care, sir! Take care! There's many a true word spoken in jest.'

'How do you mean? 'Pon my word I don't understand.'

'An old devil! The old devil, perhaps. There! Sir, you needn't laugh,' for Malcolmson had broken into a hearty peal. 'You young folks thinks it easy to laugh at things that makes older ones shudder. Never mind, sir! Never mind! Please God, you'll laugh all the time. It's what I wish you myself!' and the good lady beamed all over in sympathy with his enjoyment, her fears gone for a moment.

'Oh, forgive me!' said Malcolmson presently. 'Don't think me rude; but the idea was too much for me – that the old devil himself was on the chair last night!' And at the thought he laughed again. Then he went home to dinner.

This evening the scampering of the rats began earlier; indeed it had been going on before his arrival, and only ceased whilst his presence by its freshness disturbed them. After dinner he sat by the fire for a while and had a smoke; and then, having cleared his table, began to work as before. To-night the rats disturbed him more than they had done on the previous night. How they scampered up and down and under and over! How they squeaked, and scratched, and gnawed! How they, getting bolder by degrees, came to the mouths of their holes and to the chinks and cracks and crannies in the wainscoting till their eyes shone like tiny lamps as the firelight rose and fell. But to him, now doubtless accustomed to them, their eyes were not wicked; only their playfulness touched him. Sometimes the boldest of them made sallies out on the floor or along the mouldings of the wainscot. Now and again as they disturbed him Malcolmson made a sound to frighten them, smiting the table with his hand or giving a fierce 'Hsh, hsh,' so that they fled straightway to their holes.

And so the early part of the night wore on; and despite the noise Malcolmson got more and more immersed in his work.

All at once he stopped, as on the previous night, being overcome by a sudden sense of silence. There was not the faintest sound of gnaw, or scratch, or squeak. The silence was as of the grave. He remembered the odd occurrence of the previous night, and instinctively he looked at the chair standing close by the fireside. And then a very odd sensation thrilled through him.

There, on the great old high-backed carved oak chair beside the fireplace sat the same enormous rat, steadily glaring at him with baleful eyes.

Instinctively he took the nearest thing to his hand, a book of logarithms, and flung it at it. The book was badly aimed and the rat did not stir, so again the poker performance of the previous night was repeated; and again the rat, being closely pursued, fled up the rope of the alarm bell. Strangely too, the departure of this rat was instantly followed by the renewal of the noise made by the general rat community. On this occasion, as on the previous one, Malcolmson could not see at what part of the room the rat disappeared, for the green shade of his lamp left the upper part of the room in darkness, and the fire had burned low.

On looking at his watch he found it was close on midnight; and, not sorry for the divertissement, he made up his fire and made himself his nightly pot of tea. He had got through a good spell of work, and thought himself entitled to a cigarette; and so he sat on the great carved oak chair before the fire and enjoyed it. Whilst smoking he began to think that he would like to know where the rat disappeared to, for he had certain ideas for the morrow not entirely disconnected with a rat-trap. Accordingly he lit another lamp and placed it so that it would shine well into the right-hand corner of the wall by the fireplace. Then he got all the books he had with him, and placed them handy to throw at the vermin. Finally he lifted the rope of the alarm bell and placed the end of it on the table, fixing the extreme end under the lamp. As he handled it he could not help noticing how pliable it was, especially for so strong a rope, and one not in use. 'You could hang a man with it,' he thought to himself. When his preparations were made he looked around, and said complacently:

'There now, my friend, I think we shall learn something of you this time!' He began his work again, and though as before somewhat disturbed at first by the noise of the rats, soon lost himself in his propositions and problems.

Again he was called to his immediate surroundings suddenly. This time it might not have been the sudden silence only which took his attention; there was a slight movement of the rope, and the lamp moved. Without stirring, he looked to see if his pile of books was within range, and then cast his eye along the rope. As he looked he saw the great rat drop from the rope on the oak armchair and sit there glaring at him. He raised a book in his right hand, and taking careful aim, flung it at the rat. The latter, with a quick movement, sprang aside and dodged the missile. He then took another book, and a third, and flung them one after another at the rat, but each time unsuccessfully. At last, as he stood with a book poised in his hand to throw, the rat squeaked and seemed afraid. This made Malcolmson more than ever eager to strike, and the book flew and struck the rat a resounding blow. It gave a terrified squeak, and turning on its pursuer a look of terrible malevolence, ran up the chair-back and made a great jump to the rope of the alarm bell and ran up it like lightning. The lamp rocked under the sudden strain, but it was a heavy one and did not topple over. Malcolmson kept his eyes on the rat, and saw it by the light of the second lamp leap to a moulding of the wainscot and disappear through a hole in one of the great pictures which hung on the wall, obscured and invisible through its coating of dirt and dust.

'I shall look up my friend's habitation in the morning,' said the student, as he went over to collect his books. 'The third picture from the fireplace; I shall not forget.' He picked up the books one by one, commenting on them as he lifted them. 'Conic Sections he does not mind, nor Cycloidal Oscillations, nor the Principia, nor Quaternions, nor Thermodynamics. Now for the book that fetched him!' Malcolmson took it up and looked at it. As he did so he started, and a sudden pallor overspread his face. He looked round uneasily and shivered slightly, as he murmured to himself:

'The Bible my mother gave me! What an odd coincidence.' He sat down to work again, and the rats in the wainscot renewed their gambols. They did not disturb him, however; somehow their presence gave him a sense of companionship. But he could not attend to his work, and after striving to master the subject on which he was engaged gave it up in despair, and went to bed as the first streak of dawn stole in through the eastern window.

He slept heavily but uneasily, and dreamed much; and when Mrs Dempster woke him late in the morning he seemed ill at ease, and for a few minutes did not seem to realise exactly where he was. His first request rather surprised the servant.

'Mrs Dempster, when I am out to-day I wish you would get the steps and dust or wash those pictures – specially that one the third from the fireplace – I want to see what they are.' Late in the afternoon Malcolmson worked at his books in the shaded walk, and the cheerfulness of the previous day came back to him as the day wore on, and he found that his reading was progressing well. He had worked out to a satisfactory conclusion all the problems which had as yet baffled him, and it was in a state of jubilation that he paid a visit to Mrs Witham at 'The Good Traveller.' He found a stranger in the cosy sitting-room with the landlady, who was introduced to him as Dr Thornhill. She was not quite at ease, and this, combined with the Doctor's plunging at once into a series of questions, made Malcolmson come to the conclusion that his presence was not an accident, so without preliminary he said:

'Dr Thornhill, I shall with pleasure answer you any question you may choose to ask me if you will answer me one question first.'

The Doctor seemed surprised, but he smiled and answered at once. 'Done! What is it?' 'Did Mrs Witham ask you to come here and see me and advise me?'

Dr Thornhill for a moment was taken aback, and Mrs Witham got fiery red and turned away; but the doctor was a frank and ready man, and he answered at once and openly:

'She did: but she didn't intend you to know it. I suppose it was my clumsy haste that made you suspect. She told me that she did not like the idea of your being in that house all by yourself, and that she thought you took too much strong tea. In fact, she wants me to advise you if possible to give up the tea and the very late hours. I was a keen student in my time, so I suppose I may take the liberty of a college man, and without offence, advise you not quite as a stranger.'

Malcolmson with a bright smile held out his hand. 'Shake! As they say in America,' he said. 'I must thank you for your kindness and Mrs Witham too, and your kindness deserves a return on my part. I promise to take no more strong tea – no tea at all till you let me – and I shall go to bed to-night at one o'clock at latest. Will that do?'

'Capital,' said the Doctor. 'Now tell us all that you noticed in the old house,' and so Malcolmson then and there told in minute detail all that had happened in the last two nights. He was interrupted every now and then by some exclamation from Mrs Witham, till finally when he told of the episode of the Bible the landlady's pent-up emotions found vent in a shriek; and it was not till a stiff glass of brandy and water had been administered that she grew composed again. Dr Thornhill listened with a face of growing gravity, and when the narrative was complete and Mrs Witham had been restored he asked:

'The rat always went up the rope of the alarm bell?'

'Always.'

'I suppose you know,' said the Doctor after a pause, 'what the rope is?'

'No!'

'It is,' said the Doctor slowly, 'the very rope which the hangman used for all the victims of the Judge's judicial rancour!' Here he was interrupted by another scream from Mrs Witham, and steps had to be taken for her recovery. Malcolmson having looked at his watch, and found that it was close to his dinner hour, had gone home before her complete recovery.

When Mrs Witham was herself again she almost assailed the Doctor with angry questions as to what he meant by putting such horrible ideas into the poor young man's mind. 'He has quite enough there already to upset him,' she added. Dr Thornhill replied:

'My dear madam, I had a distinct purpose in it! I wanted to draw his attention to the bell rope, and to fix it there. It may be that he is in a highly overwrought state, and has been studying too much, although I am bound to say that he seems as sound and healthy a young man, mentally and bodily, as ever I saw – but then the rats – and that suggestion of the devil.' The doctor shook his head and went on. 'I would have offered to go and stay the first night with him but that I felt sure it would have been a cause of offence. He may get in the night some strange fright or hallucination; and if he does I want him to pull that rope. All alone as he is it will give us warning, and we may reach him in time to be of service. I shall be sitting up pretty late to-night and shall keep my ears open. Do not be alarmed if Benchurch gets a surprise before morning.'

'Oh, Doctor, what do you mean? What do you mean?'

'I mean this; that possibly – nay, more probably – we shall hear the great alarm bell from the Judge's House to-night,' and the Doctor made about as effective an exit as could be thought of.

When Malcolmson arrived home he found that it was a little after his usual time, and Mrs Dempster had gone away – the rules of Greenhow's Charity were not to be neglected. He was glad to see that the place was bright and tidy with a cheerful fire and a well-trimmed lamp. The evening was colder than might have been expected in April, and a heavy wind was blowing with such rapidly-increasing strength that there was every promise of a storm during the night. For a few minutes after his entrance the noise of the rats ceased; but so soon as they became accustomed to his presence they began again. He was glad to hear them, for he felt once more the feeling of companionship in their noise, and his mind ran back to the strange fact that they only ceased to manifest themselves when that other – the great rat with the baleful eyes – came upon the scene. The reading-lamp only was lit and its green shade kept the ceiling and the upper part of the room in darkness, so that the cheerful light from the hearth spreading over the floor and shining on the white cloth laid over the end of the table was warm and cheery. Malcolmson sat down to his dinner with a good appetite and a buoyant spirit. After his dinner and a cigarette he sat steadily down to work, determined not to let anything disturb him, for he remembered his promise to the doctor, and made up his mind to make the best of the time at his disposal.

For an hour or so he worked all right, and then his thoughts began to wander from his books. The actual circumstances around him, the calls on his physical attention, and his nervous susceptibility were not to be denied. By this time the wind had become a gale, and the gale a storm. The old house, solid though it was, seemed to shake to its foundations, and the storm roared and raged through its many chimneys and its queer old gables, producing strange, unearthly sounds in the empty rooms and corridors. Even the great alarm bell on the roof must have felt the force of the wind, for the rope rose and fell slightly, as though the bell were moved a little from time to time, and the limber rope fell on the oak floor with a hard and hollow sound.

As Malcolmson listened to it he bethought himself of the doctor's words, 'It is the rope which the hangman used for the victims of the Judge's judicial rancour,' and he went over to the corner of the fireplace and took it in his hand to look at it. There seemed a sort of deadly interest in it, and as he stood there he lost himself for a moment in speculation as to who these victims were, and the grim wish of the Judge to have such a ghastly relic ever under his eyes. As he stood there the swaying of the bell on the roof still lifted the rope now and again; but presently there came a new sensation – a sort of tremor in the rope, as though something was moving along it.

Looking up instinctively Malcolmson saw the great rat coming slowly down towards him, glaring at him steadily. He dropped the rope and started back with a muttered curse, and the rat turning ran up the rope again and disappeared, and at the same instant Malcolmson became conscious that the noise of the rats, which had ceased for a while, began again.

All this set him thinking, and it occurred to him that he had not investigated the lair of the rat or looked at the pictures, as he had intended. He lit the other lamp without the shade, and, holding it up, went and stood opposite the third picture from the fireplace on the right-hand side where he had seen the rat disappear on the previous night.

At the first glance he started back so suddenly that he almost dropped the lamp, and a deadly pallor overspread his face. His knees shook, and heavy drops of sweat came on his forehead, and he trembled like an aspen. But he was young and plucky, and pulled himself together, and after the pause of a few seconds stepped forward again, raised the lamp, and examined the picture which had been dusted and washed, and now stood out clearly.

It was of a judge dressed in his robes of scarlet and ermine. His face was strong and merciless, evil, crafty, and vindictive, with a sensual mouth, hooked nose of ruddy colour, and shaped like the beak of a bird of prey. The rest of the face was of a cadaverous colour. The eyes were of peculiar brilliance and with a terribly malignant expression. As he looked at them, Malcolmson grew cold, for he saw there the very counterpart of the eyes of the great rat. The lamp almost fell from his hand, he saw the rat with its baleful eyes peering out through the hole in the corner of the picture, and noted the sudden cessation of the noise of the other rats. However, he pulled himself together, and went on with his examination of the picture. The Judge was seated in a great high-backed carved oak chair, on the right-hand side of a great stone fireplace where, in the corner, a rope hung down from the ceiling, its end lying coiled on the floor. With a feeling of something like horror, Malcolmson recognised the scene of the room as it stood, and gazed around him in an awe-struck manner as though he expected to find some strange presence behind him. Then he looked over to the corner of the fireplace – and with a loud cry he let the lamp fall from his hand.

There, in the Judge's arm-chair, with the rope hanging behind, sat the rat with the Judge's baleful eyes, now intensified and with a fiendish leer. Save for the howling of the storm without there was silence.

The fallen lamp recalled Malcolmson to himself. Fortunately it was of metal, and so the oil was not spilt. However, the practical need of attending to it settled at once his nervous apprehensions. When he had turned it out, he wiped his brow and thought for a moment.

'This will not do,' he said to himself. 'If I go on like this I shall become a crazy fool. This must stop! I promised the Doctor I would not take tea. Faith, he was pretty right! My nerves must have been getting into a queer state. Funny I did not notice it. I never felt better in my life. However, it is all right now, and I shall not be such a fool again.'

Then he mixed himself a good stiff glass of brandy and water and resolutely sat down to his work.

It was nearly an hour when he looked up from his book, disturbed by the sudden stillness. Without, the wind howled and roared louder than ever, and the rain drove in sheets against the windows, beating like hail on the glass; but within there was no sound whatever save the echo of the wind as it roared in the great chimney, and now and then a hiss as a few raindrops found their way down the chimney in a lull of the storm. The fire had fallen low and had ceased to flame, though it threw out a red glow. Malcolmson listened attentively, and presently heard a thin, squeaking noise, very faint. It came from the corner of the room where the rope hung down, and he thought it was the creaking of the rope on the floor as the swaying of the bell raised and lowered it. Looking up, however, he saw in the dim light the great rat clinging to the rope and gnawing it. The rope was already nearly gnawed through – he could see the lighter colour where the strands were laid bare. As he looked the job was completed, and the severed end of the rope fell clattering on the oaken floor, whilst for an instant the great rat remained like a knob or tassel at the end of the rope, which now began to sway to and fro. Malcolmson felt for a moment another pang of terror as he thought that now the possibility of calling the outer world to his assistance was cut off, but an intense anger took its place, and seizing the book he was reading he hurled it at the rat. The blow was well aimed, but before the missile could reach it the rat dropped off and struck the floor with a soft thud. Malcolmson instantly rushed over towards it, but it darted away and disappeared in the darkness of the shadows of the room. Malcolmson felt that his work was over for the night, and determined then and there to vary the monotony of the proceedings by a hunt for the rat, and took off the green shade of the lamp so as to insure a wider spreading light. As he did so the gloom of the upper part of the room was relieved, and in the new flood of light, great by comparison with the previous darkness, the pictures on the wall stood out boldly. From where he stood, Malcolmson saw right opposite to him the third picture on the wall from the right of the fireplace. He rubbed his eyes in surprise, and then a great fear began to come upon him.

In the centre of the picture was a great irregular patch of brown canvas, as fresh as when it was stretched on the frame. The background was as before, with chair and chimney-corner and rope, but the figure of the Judge had disappeared.

Malcolmson, almost in a chill of horror, turned slowly round, and then he began to shake and tremble like a man in a palsy. His strength seemed to have left him, and he was incapable of action or movement, hardly even of thought. He could only see and hear.

There, on the great high-backed carved oak chair sat the Judge in his robes of scarlet and ermine, with his baleful eyes glaring vindictively, and a smile of triumph on the resolute, cruel mouth, as he lifted with his hands a black cap. Malcolmson felt as if the blood was running from his heart, as one does in moments of prolonged suspense. There was a singing in his ears. Without, he could hear the roar and howl of the tempest, and through it, swept on the storm, came the striking of midnight by the great chimes in the market place. He stood for a space of time that seemed to him endless, still as a statue and with wide-open, horror-struck eyes, breathless. As the clock struck, so the smile of triumph on the Judge's face intensified, and at the last stroke of midnight he placed the black cap on his head.

Slowly and deliberately the Judge rose from his chair and picked up the piece of the rope of the alarm bell which lay on the floor, drew it through his hands as if he enjoyed its touch, and then deliberately began to knot one end of it, fashioning it into a noose. This he tightened and tested with his foot, pulling hard at it till he was satisfied and then making a running noose of it, which he held in his hand. Then he began to move along the table on the opposite side to Malcolmson, keeping his eyes on him until he had passed him, when with a quick movement he stood in front of the door. Malcolmson then began to feel that he was trapped, and tried to think of what he should do. There was some fascination in the Judge's eyes, which he never took off him, and he had, perforce, to look. He saw the Judge approach – still keeping between him and the door – and raise the noose and throw it towards him as if to entangle him. With a great effort he made a quick movement to one side, and saw the rope fall beside him, and heard it strike the oaken floor. Again the Judge raised the noose and tried to ensnare him, ever keeping his baleful eyes fixed on him, and each time by a mighty effort the student just managed to evade it. So this went on for many times, the Judge seeming never discouraged nor discomposed at failure, but playing as a cat does with a mouse. At last in despair, which had reached its climax, Malcolmson cast a quick glance round him. The lamp seemed to have blazed up, and there was a fairly good light in the room. At the many rat-holes and in the chinks and crannies of the wainscot he saw the rats' eyes; and this aspect, that was purely physical, gave him a gleam of comfort. He looked around and saw that the rope of the great alarm bell was laden with rats. Every inch of it was covered with them, and more and more were pouring through the small circular hole in the ceiling whence it emerged, so that with their weight the bell was beginning to sway.

Hark! It had swayed till the clapper had touched the bell. The sound was but a tiny one, but the bell was only beginning to sway, and it would increase.

At the sound the Judge, who had been keeping his eyes fixed on Malcolmson, looked up, and a scowl of diabolical anger overspread his face. His eyes fairly glowed like hot coals, and he stamped his foot with a sound that seemed to make the house shake. A dreadful peal of thunder broke overhead as he raised the rope again, whilst the rats kept running up and down the rope as though working against time. This time, instead of throwing it, he drew close to his victim, and held open the noose as he approached. As he came closer there seemed something paralysing in his very presence, and Malcolmson stood rigid as a corpse. He felt the Judge's icy fingers touch his throat as he adjusted the rope. The noose tightened – tightened. Then the Judge, taking the rigid form of the student in his arms, carried him over and placed him standing in the oak chair, and stepping up beside him, put his hand up and caught the end of the swaying rope of the alarm bell. As he raised his hand the rats fled squeaking, and disappeared through the hole in the ceiling. Taking the end of the noose which was round Malcolmson's neck he tied it to the hanging bell-rope, and then descending, pulled away the chair.

When the alarm bell of the Judge's House began to sound a crowd soon assembled. Lights and torches of various kinds appeared, and soon a silent crowd was hurrying to the spot. They knocked loudly at the door, but there was no reply. Then they burst in the door, and poured into the great dining-room, the doctor at the head.

There at the end of the rope of the great alarm bell hung the body of the student, and on the face of the Judge in the picture was a malignant smile.

ABOUT DACRE STOKER

Dacre Stoker is the great grand-nephew of Bram Stoker and the international best-selling co-author of *Dracula the Un-Dead* (2009), the Stoker family endorsed sequel to *Dracula*. Dacre is also the co-editor (with Elizabeth Miller) of *The Lost Journal of Bram Stoker: The Dublin Years* (2012). Released in October of 2018, *Dracul,* a prequel to *Dracula,* co-authored with JD Barker, was the UK's # 1 Bestselling Hardcover Novel in Horror and Supernatural in 2018, and a top 5 finalist by the Horror Writers Association for the Bram Stoker Award for Superior Achievement in a Novel. Film rights for *Dracul* have been optioned by Paramount Studios.

Dacre's recent work includes *Dracula's Bedlam* (2021) with Chris McAuley and John Peel and *The Virgin's Embrace* (2021) with Chris McAuley. Additionally, short stories with Leverett Butts, 'Last Days', appeared in *Weird Tales* Magazine, 'The Tired Captain', featured in *FX Sherlock Holmes Anthology*, 'Enter the Dragon' in Classic Monsters Unleashed Anthology and 'The Lost Warrior', in the anthology *Dracula UnFanged.*

A native of Montreal, Canada, Dacre taught Physical Education and Sciences for twenty-two years, in both Canada and the US. He participated in the sport of Modern Pentathlon as an athlete and a coach at the international and Olympic levels for Canada for 12 years. He is also an avid player and coach of the unique game of Real Tennis. In May of 2016 an athlete he had been coaching for the past 4 years, Camden Riviere, won the World Championships of Court Tennis.

Dacre has consulted and appeared in recent film documentaries about vampires in literature and popular culture: *The Real Vampire Files* (2010 History Channel), *The Tillinghast Nightmare,* (2014 Historical Haunts), *Secrets of the Dead* (2015 PBS), *Mysteries at the Museum,* (2017 Travel Channel), and *Legend Hunter* (2019 Travel Channel). He currently hosts tours to Dublin, Whitby, and Cruden Bay, to visit places where Bram Stoker lived, was educated, worked, researched, and wrote *Dracula.* He also leads groups to Transylvania to explore both the life and times of the historic Vlad Dracula III and also the locations where Bram Stoker set his famous novel.

ALSO PUBLISHED BY TELOS PUBLISHING

<u>BRAM STOKER</u>
DRACULA – 125th Anniversary Edition

<u>SAM STONE (aka Samantha Lee Howe)</u>
THE VAMPIRE GENE
Horror, thriller, time-travel series.
1: KILLING KISS
2: FUTILE FLAME
3: DEMON DANCE
4: HATEFUL HEART
5: SILENT SAND
6: JADED JEWEL

JINX CHRONICLES
Hi–tech science fiction fantasy series
1: JINX TOWN
2: JINX MAGIC
3: JINX BOUND
THE JINX CHRONICLES

KAT LIGHTFOOT MYSTERIES
Steampunk, horror, adventure series
1: ZOMBIES AT TIFFANY'S
2: KAT ON A HOT TIN AIRSHIP
3: WHAT'S DEAD PUSSYKAT
4: KAT OF GREEN TENTACLES
5: KAT AND THE PENDULUM
6: TEN LITTLE DEMONS
THE COMPLETE LIGHTFOOT

THE DARKNESS WITHIN
Science Fiction Horror Short Novel

CTHULHU AND OTHER MONSTERS
ZOMBIES IN NEW YORK AND OTHER BLOODY JOTTINGS
LEGENDS OF CTHULHU AND OTHER NIGHTMARES
Short story collections

<u>BRYONY PEARCE</u>
WAVEFUNCTION
WINDRUNNER'S DAUGHTER

<u>TANITH LEE</u>
TANITH LEE A TO Z
BLOOD 20
DEATH OF THE DAY

<u>STEPHEN LAWS</u>
SPECTRE

<u>SIMON CLARK</u>
THE FALL
HUMPTY'S BONES

<u>HELEN MCCABE</u>
THE PIPER TRILOGY
1: PIPER
2: THE PIERCING
3: THE CODEX

<u>RAVEN DANE</u>
ABSINTHE AND ARSENIC
DEATH'S DARK WINGS

THE MISADVENTURES OF CYRUS DARIAN
Steampunk Series
CYRUS DARIAN AND THE TECHNOMICRON
CYRUS DARIAN AND THE GHASTLY HORDE
CYRUS DARIAN AND THE WICKED WRAITH

PAUL FINCH
CAPE WRATH & THE HELLION
TERROR TALES OF CORNWALL (Editor)
TERROR TALES OF NORTHWEST ENGLAND (Editor)
TERROR TALES OF THE SCOTTISH LOWLANDS (Editor)

SOLOMON STRANGE
THE HAUNTING OF GOSPALL

FIONA ANGWIN
HUNTED BY DEMONS

DAVID J HOWE
TALESPINNING

FREDA WARRINGTON
NIGHTS OF BLOOD WINE

PAUL LEWIS
SMALL GHOSTS

DAWN G HARRIS
DIVINER

STEVE LOCKLEY & PAUL LEWIS
KING OF ALL THE DEAD

SIMON MORDEN
ANOTHER WAR

GRAHAM MASTERTON
THE HELL CANDIDATE
THE DJINN
RULES OF DUEL (WITH WILLIAM S BURROUGHS)
THE WELLS OF HELL

TELOS PUBLISHING
www.telos.co.uk

* 9 7 8 1 8 4 5 8 3 2 0 2 5 *